W9-AQT-054

studies in art series

Modern Art: The Nineteenth and Twentieth Centuries

John C. Galloway

Modern Art:
The Nineteenth and
Twentieth Centuries

studies in art series

Modern Art: The Nineteenth and Twentieth Centuries

John Galloway
Oakland University
Rochester, Michigan

WM. C. BROWN COMPANY PUBLISHERS
Dubuque, Iowa

STUDIES IN ART SERIES

Consulting Editor

WILLARD F. WANKELMAN
Bowling Green University

A growing interest in art and art history is evident today in the United States and has created a need for a new approach in the formulation of classroom teaching materials.

The STUDIES IN ART SERIES, designed for introductory courses in art appreciation and art history, transmits the excitement of the subject to the student seeking a liberal education. This series offers both the student and teacher flexibility of subject matter as well as authoritative writing in each topic area. Although the individual titles are self-contained, collectively they cover the major subjects usually discussed in an introductory course.

Copyright © 1967 by
Wm. C. Brown Company Publishers

Library of Congress Catalog Card Number: 67–22713

Printed in United States of America

THIRD PRINTING, 1968

preface

This book is intended to afford all readers a compressed history and interpretation of the major trends of nineteenth and twentieth century painting and sculpture. It is especially written for students in courses in art history, art education, and art appreciation offered by college departments and schools of fine arts and is meant to serve both as a guide to modern art and as a supplement to existing broad surveys of art history and other general textbooks in its field.

Modern painting and sculpture have won increasingly great prestige among contemporary people of all stations and backgrounds and in all parts of the world. General readers as well as college and art school students will find it rewarding to familiarize themselves with the art forms of the present day and the recent past as these are presented in stylistic and historical context. Hopefully, this small book will direct its audience with increased confidence to confront the originals of the works which it surveys.

Effort has been made to provide cogent art historical data as well as compact interpretation of all major movements in art of the period here discussed.

* * * * * * *

Small as this book is, it owes much to the ideas and cooperation of many persons. The bibliography lists numerous publications to whose authors I am indebted. I am deeply obliged to my former teachers at Columbia University, especially Professor Meyer Schapiro and Professor Paul Wingert, and to my colleagues Professor John B. Cameron and Professor John L. Beardman at Oakland University. The officials and staff members of various museums and galleries, as well as several private collectors, have given kind assistance by granting access to their collections and by cooperating in the procurement of photographs and permission to reproduce them.

I express my warm thanks to each of these persons and particularly to my wife, who has patiently worked with me on all manner of detail.

Oakland University   John Galloway
Rochester, Michigan

contents

The Nineteenth Century:
DAVID TO COURBET

When we speak of modern art, most of us are thinking of paintings and sculptures which reveal more than likeness or story telling. The images which come to our minds may be representational or abstract, appealing or shocking, vividly or somberly colored; but each of them denotes the artist's conceptual power and capacity to create special order for natural forms or to discover unseen ones.

Modern art emerged from a lengthy genesis. Its characteristics appear in certain ancient, primitive, and medieval works. But its proper ambiance is the nineteenth and early twentieth centuries, when, in greater numbers than before, artists realized that their forms and techniques were not subservient to nature and narrative. The styles of nineteenth century art, with which we begin our study, were often obscured by thematic veils of political or literary innuendo. The two movements which dominated European and American painting and sculpture between 1780 and 1850, Neoclassicism and Romanticism, contributed to the modern tradition, although their typical masterpieces do not at once seem to be in character.

NEOCLASSICISM

Neoclassical works often bore titles taken from Greek and Roman literature. Kings and revolutionaries alike commissioned the painting of allegories with whose ancient heroes they felt moral identity. Romantic art, often contrasted to neoclassical art, shared with the latter the depiction of grandiose subjects which had been, or might better have been, described in verbal media. Yet each of the two movements left great works whose qualities of structure are not overwhelmed by their noble and dramatic themes. Some of these monuments disclose an affinity with recent modern style.

The French neoclassicist Jacques Louis David (1748–1825) created such examples. The manner of his paintings was based upon an incisive study of Greek and Roman works which, as a winner of the Royal Academy's Prix de Rome scholarship, David saw in Italy. His great historical canvases, such as *The Oath of the Horatii* of 1784 and *The Death of Socrates* (Fig. 1), both painted shortly before the French revolution, have been interpreted to imply, in their stern moral idealism, indictment of the lubricity of Louis XVI's court and prediction of revolutionary virtues. But such analogies, although they are appealing and convenient to the broad study of late eighteenth-century history, are risky. David's remarkably lucid style, as well as his idealistic subject, express a firm order which was notably absent in the terror-soaked régimes which followed the overthrow of Louis XVI in 1789. *The Oath of the Horatii* and *The Death of Socrates* should, in that connection, have been painted somewhat later when Napoleon established a government whose resoluteness resembled that of David's art.

It is interesting, too, that the story of the heroism of Socrates is not self-evident in this masterpiece. Neither the courage of the great Athenian philosopher in choosing death by poison rather than renouncing his subversive convictions, nor the fact that his cup contains poison

Figure 1. Jacques Louis David. *The Death of Socrates*, 1787. 51 × 77¼". (The Metropolitan Museum of Art, New York. Wolfe Fund, 1931.)

Figure 2. Jacques Louis David. *The Coronation of Napoleon,* 1808. 240 × 366½". (The Louvre, Paris.)

instead of another beverage, nor even the general situation, is manifest in the actual forms of this remarkable painting. We must be verbally instructed to know the contents.

If, however, we call this canvas *Painting, 1787* and briefly set aside its literary values in favor of closely examining its great stylistic integrity, we may observe that David was a master of formal organization. He has established, in a surprisingly modern declaration, a powerful, vector-like horizontal movement whose figures relate to one another and to architectural elements in the background. Subtle repetitions of curves and angles extend both laterally and in successive planes in depth, and sensitive manipulation of lighting further unifies the different zones of David's composition. Both older and more recent artists, from the French baroque master Poussin to the neoimpressionist Seurat and the cubist Picasso, have used similar horizontal motifs; but none of them was more persuasive in its application than is David in *The Death of Socrates.*

The Coronation of Napoleon (Fig. 2) is an enormous picture whose awesome, internationally significant subject caused David to make hundreds of preparatory sketches and portraits as well as a detailed scale model of Notre Dame Cathedral in Paris, where the ceremony took place. It is easy to overlook the artist's fundamental design in this canvas because of the infinite detail of its particulars and our under-standable urge to seek out major and lesser identities. But David has again used a horizontal ordering of the main grouping of forms, this time adding the drama of a spatial canopy overhead. A less sensitive neoclassical or romantic artist might have enhanced the excitement of this narrative by strongly accenting the figures of Napoleon and Jose-phine, but David makes them only slightly more prominent than the figures surrounding them and unites their images with the subtle flow of light. The astonishing breadth of the basic composition and lighting assimilates the realistic details of the scores of faces and costumes.

David was equally masterful in his handling of smaller, individual portrait and figure paintings; but it is in the formalized, large-scale allegorical and historical paintings that we see his full strength and imagination.

David's contribution to the history of French art is unique. A prestigious and ardent revolutionist, he reorganized the Academy, sponsored the support of museums and art schools, and expanded the collections of the Louvre. He was autocratic in the administration of the Institute of Fine Arts, but deeply gifted as a teacher.[1] His great-est achievement, however, was his acceleration and refinement of the neoclassical style, within whose austere limits he was able to assert far more than the imitation of nature and the narration of classic and historic themes.

The fall of Napoleon's empire and the return of the Bourbon Dynasty forced David, a regicide of Louis XVI and Marie Antoinette, into exile in Brussels from 1816 until his death, in 1825. His strong leadership at the Institute temporarily passed to Napoleon's favorite portrait painter, Baron Antoine-Jean Gros (discussed later in connection with romanticism). It was not until another of David's protegés, Jean Dominique Ingres, became director of fine arts that Neoclassicism found an ardently partisan advocate.

Meanwhile, the movement known as Romanticism was gaining force; and, headed by the brilliant Eugène Delacroix, it sharply chal-lenged the supremacy of the older style. Many painters who had been trained in the neoclassical manner had hovered between David's re-strained, finished method and the new vigor and restlessness of roman-ticism. Among them was Anne-Louis Girodet, one of David's Prix de Rome students, whose style actually remained neoclassical but whose themes show the romantic trend toward contemporaneous literature, such as Chauteaubriand's pietistic, primitivizing subjects and Gaelic legends. Jean-Baptiste Regnault, Pierre-Narcisse Guérin, Baron Francois-

Pascal Gérard, Pierre-Paul Prud'hon, and Marie-Guilhelmine Benoist also felt certain affinities for the romantic attitude without remarkably changing from their neoclassicist background.

Jean Auguste Dominique Ingres (1780–1867) was the proper successor of David, a singularly talented but autocratic individual, whose leadership at the Institute and its Ecole des Beaux Arts withstood the challenge of Delacroix and the romantics and, unfortunately, carried neoclassicism many years beyond its reasonable historical limits. A product of David's own studio and winner of the Prix de Rome, Ingres on two occasions spent many years in Italian residence, but soon after 1824 he became in effect the dictator of fine arts in France and was even more prestigious internationally than had been his master. Ingres' *The Vow of Louis XIII,* which won him unlimited praise from academicians at the 1824 official Salon exhibition, was more nearly based upon high renaissance sources and Ingres' own peculiarly sharp, linear ideals than upon classical or Davidian norms. He believed that his vast historical canvases, which he intended to excel those of David, would assure his future renown; but the searching, elegant portraits which he looked upon chiefly as a mere source of income are now regarded as his finest works. Ingres' likeness of the *Comtesse d'Haussonville* (Fig. 3) is an especially appealing example.[2] This picture has been criticized for its great detail, but Ingres' minute rendering of particulars of the reflected forms and other secondary elements actually provides a subtle foil for the broader, relaxed treatment of the subject's face and arms. The masterfully painted folds of the dress act as vertical notes echoing in the severer lines of the mirror and corner moulding. As in David's art, stylistic clarity and subtlety are present beneath the more immediately engaging content which they convey.

Ingres, in spite of his conflict with Delacroix and other romantic artists, sometimes used the exotic subjects which they introduced. Near-East harem scenes and reclining odalisques (in which a face appeared copied almost literally by Ingres from a Raphael painting) were among such un-neoclassical themes. Unlike the romantics, most of whom painted with a certain brokenness and sweep of color and line, Ingres insisted upon a continuous, clear-cut linearity and severely muted color. His figures were only slightly modeled, and his compositions lacked the vigorous dark and light contrasts present in much romantic painting.

So massive was Ingres' prestige and authority that even the most talented of his followers felt a certain lack of confidence in their abilities. Hippolyte Delaroche and Théodore Chassériau, for example, were remarkably competent technicians, but the shadow of Ingres appears to

Figure 3. Jean-Auguste Dominique Ingres, *Comtesse d'-
Haussonville*, 1845. (Copyright The Frick Collection, New
York.)

have prevented their developing a singular style or fully converting to
the romantic movement, with which they felt sympathy. One of the least
admirable effects of Ingres' administration of the Institute was the
rigidity of his Salon juries. This periodic exhibition was not only the
official showplace of acceptable painting and sculpture, but also an
institution which assured professional and economic distinction or
oblivion. During the many decades of Ingres' authority, the Salon
rarely admitted the works of artists who were not clearly neoclassical
or otherwise acceptable to the academic norm. Among the approved,
medal- and Prix de Rome-winning artists were Horace Vernet, François
Joseph Heim, Alexandre Cabanel, Hippolyte Flandrin, Alexandre-
Gabriel Descamps, Carolus Duran, Léon Cogniet, Jean Louis Ernest
Meissonier, Joseph Robert Fleury, and a host of other successful
academicians whose slick variant of Neoclassicism no longer commands
critical respect. The Salon, which had been established in 1648 with
the advent of the French Royal Academy of artists, became by the
middle of the nineteenth century a symbol of conservatism.

One of the few essentially neoclassical painters who developed
a personal expression was Pierre Puvis de Chavannes (1824–1898). He

is hard to fit into the stylistic pattern of his time. Like Ingres, he was influenced by Italian renaissance painting; but his manner was less severe. Renowned for his huge murals in French cathedrals and secular buildings, Puvis also painted smaller easel works, such as *The Prodigal Son* (Fig. 4), which are saturated with a hushed, private mood. It is to be noted that several postimpressionist painters including Van Gogh and Seurat, respected the art of this uncharacteristic neoclassicist.

ROMANTICISM

The conflicts between the romantics and the neoclassicists are often exaggerated and sometimes inaccurately defined.[3] Much of the discord was personal as well as professional and resulted from the control of the school of fine arts and the annual Salon by the academic neoclassicists. Stylistically, the chief difference between the two factions was not so much the comparatively strong romantic color as against the tonal light-and-dark linearity of the academy, so often stressed in

Figure 4. Pierre Puvis de Chavannes. *The Prodigal Son,* c. 1878. 41¾ × 58″. (National Gallery of Art, Washington, D. C. Chester Dale Collection.)

critical interpretations, but the vigorous, sweeping brushwork and overall restlessness of the younger group. Their compositions, too, often
affirmed their admiration of such baroque masters as Rubens, whose
diagonal and other motifs were compatible with their dynamic concepts and relatively spontaneous approach to art. Delacroix and his
adherents, like the neoclassicists, frequently turned to literary sources
for their themes; but the former preferred Shakespeare and Dante, along
with such contemporaries as Goethe, Byron, and Sir Walter Scott, to
classical mythology and history. North Africa provided exotic subjects.

Baron Antoine-Jean Gros (1771–1835) was the first neoclassically
trained artist of major stature to turn romantic, although it is true that
he never fully did so and that he might better be called a romantic
neoclassicist. It has been mentioned that he was Napoleon's favorite
portrait painter. He also made such historical canvases of Napoleon's
campaigns as *Napoleon among the Plague-Stricken at Jaffa* (Fig. 5),
depending, as usually, upon careful reports by eyewitnesses rather than
upon being present. This painting, which shows that Gros felt pulled
toward both neoclassical and romantic ideals, shows an early use of
orientalizing motifs, such as the architectural details of the building

Figure 5. Antoine-Jean Gros. *Napoleon among the Plague-Stricken at Jaffa*, 1804(?). (The Louvre, Paris.)

Figure 6. Théodore Géricault. Study for *Raft of the Medusa,* 1819
(16′ 1″ × 23′ 6″). (The Louvre, Paris.)

which has been converted into a pesthouse for the afflicted soldiers.
The emperor is depicted in a savior-like role, unafraid of the disease
which surrounds him and consoling the stricken troops.

Théodore Géricault (1791–1824), who exhibited only three major
works during his brief but significant career, was the first distinctively
romantic painter. His works of 1812 already displayed the rippling
brushwork and diagonalized composition which are so characteristic of
the romantic style. Géricault was also one of the exemplars of romantic
choice of themes, often using such bizarre subjects as heads of guillo-
tined men. He also painted a remarkable and sympathetic series of
portraits of mental patients at the Hôspital Salpêtrière.[4] Géricault's celebrated *Raft of the Medusa* (Fig. 6, sketch) created a sensation at the
Salon of 1819 not only because of its romantic vigor of style but also
because of its political import. The commander of the ship *Medusa,*
whose incompetence and cowardice led to his vessel's wreck and the
subsequent seizure of lifeboats by the officers and passengers, was a

fugitive from the revolution who had been restored by the Bourbon dynasty. Géricault's use of this topical incident, which led to the abandonment of the ship's crew on overcrowded rafts and to agonized privations and scores of deaths, accelerated the current disfavor of the new monarchy. Showing influence by mannerist and Caravaggesque painting, this stirring work is another document of early romantic style.

Eugène Delacroix (1798–1863) was not only leader of the romantics but was outstanding in the entire intellectual design of Paris from the 1820s until midcentury. His admirers included the brillant poet-critic, Charles Baudelaire, whose support was integral to the romantic cause. Trained as a neoclassicist, Delacroix transcended his background but did not think of himself as a revolutionary. He was, he thought, a true classicist who brought to that tradition a new vigor and liberation. Although Delacroix was refused admission to membership in the Academy until late in his career, he nevertheless received many important official commissions. It is believed on substantive grounds that his natural father was the famous statesman Talleyrand; and this might account for his becoming a renowned and widely favored artist despite his conflict with Ingres and his faction.

Delacroix, like Géricault, contributed to the modern tradition a refreshing boldness of design and brushwork. His study of color theory in the writings of Michel-Eugène Chevreul and other scientists, and, more importantly, his revival of the bright tones used by Rubens and the Venetian painters, was revelant to later, more modern exploitations of the medium. The neoimpressionist painter and theorist Paul Signac admired Delacroix for eliminating muddy tones from his shadows, substituting for them purer shades of blue and violet, and for accelerating the power of reds, for example, by placing greens adjacently. Typical neoclassical color had been based upon the relation of dark and light modulations of tones, with little emphasis upon pure or saturate hues. Delacroix appears to have first been stimulated in this interest by the British landscapes of John Constable which he saw in 1824.

The subjects painted by Delacroix typify romantic interests: themes from Dante's *Inferno,* Shakespeare's *Hamlet,* Byron's *Don Juan,* Scott's novels, Goethe's works, current historical episodes from the Turkish war against the Greeks, and various exotic topics from Algiers and the Arabian desert, such as wild animal hunts and odalisques in picturesque costumes. One of Delacroix's most dramatic compositions is *The Barricade* (*Liberty Leading the People*) (Fig. 7), a document of the revolution of 1830 which deposed the Bourbon monarchy and brought to the throne Louis Philippe, the "citizen king." The great excitement of this masterpiece of romanticism is powerfully ordered by Delacroix in

Figure 7. Eugène Delacroix. *The Barricade (Liberty Leading the People),* 1830. 8′ 6″ × 10′ 8″. (The Louvre, Paris.)

a design which makes active almost all sectors of the canvas. Its emotionally charged atmosphere is so sensitively interpreted by the painter that other than visual senses are invoked (a characteristic of certain German expressionist works of the early twentieth century). Noise and the smell of exploded powder are almost as sharply suggested as are the visual forms of *The Barricade.*

Talents so obviously great as those of Delacroix, Géricault, Gros, and other romantics became influential throughout Europe and in the United States in spite of their general lack of official academic approval.

Meanwhile, an extraordinary Spanish independent, Francisco de Goya (1746–1828), who was never significantly impressed by neoclassical ideals, founded his own romantic expression. Goya was many things at once: a romantic, a realist, a painter of demonic fantasies, a singularly gifted printmaker, and leading court artist of the Spanish monarchy. Although the German artist Anton Raphael Mengs and the distinguished Giovanni Battisto Tiepolo of Italy were influential in Spain, Goya's style was uniquely personal. As court painter, Goya was at least as

Figure 8. Francisco de Goya. *The Shootings of May 3, 1808 at Madrid*, 1814. 8′ 9″ × 13′ 4″. (Museo del Prado, Madrid.)

politically opportunistic as his exact contemporary, David. Much as he loathed the Napoleonic forces which invaded and occupied Spain, Goya painted the portraits of French dignitaries; and, with the restoration of the Spanish monarchy, he once again became the favorite court artist. Goya was singularly devoted to his art, and if he was astonishingly candid in his portraits of Spanish royalty, he was equally pitiless in his self-portraits and in his renowned series of etchings, *The Caprices,* which bitingly depicted the falseness and stupidity of various kinds of people.

Goya's humanity was best characterized by his hatred of war and the bestialities that attend it. His etchings called *The Disasters of War,* created around 1813–1815 but not published until about 1820, are a scathing denunciation not only of the French military who slaughtered and pillaged during their occupation of Spain, but of armed brutality in general. Goya's intensely dramatic *The Shootings of May 3, 1808, at Madrid* (Fig. 8) rivals Delacroix's *The Barricade* as a romantic monument to human aggressiveness, Goya's being a record of extreme negation. The violence of its theme is beautifully matched by Goya's conceptual and technical handling of light, movement, and the agonizingly tense interval between gun muzzles and victims.

By way of contrast, Goya's smallish ink-and-wash drawing, *Evil Counsel* (Fig. 9), shows his great power as a draftsman even in reduced scale. Goya, who insisted that he saw no lines in nature, was nevertheless an outstanding master of draftsmanship.

This Spanish artist rivals any other contemporary as a contributor to the romantic movement, and he was an antecedent of the modern spirit of invention and dedication.

Romantic art in most parts of Europe impelled new and diverse subjects as well as bold innovations in style. Landscape painting, which had been relegated by the old Royal Academy in France to a low category of approved subjects, won great recognition during the 1830s and later, especially among a middle-class purchasing public. French artists from Claude Lorrain and Nicolas Poussin to the rococo masters Boucher and Fragonard had usually introduced the human figure (even if often in a subsidiary role) into their outdoor scenes. Pierre-Henri de Valenciennes and François Marius Granet, however, often

Figure 9. Francisco de Goya. *Evil Counsel,* c. 1805. Ink wash drawing, 10 × 6¾". (The Phillips Collection, Washington, D. C.)

painted landscapes without figures, anticipating the practice of the long-unheralded but now celebrated Barbizon group of landscapists who centered, partly because of economic necessity, in the town of that name near the Fontainebleau forest. The Barbizonists and their leader, Théodore Rousseau (1812–1867), were strongly impressed by the Dutch landscapes of such seventeenth-century masters as Van de Velde, Jan van Goyen, Jacob van Ruisdael, and Albert Cuyp, rather than by French, Italian, or English sources. Rousseau, Jules Dupré, Diaz de la Peña, Charles Daubigny, and Jean François Millet founded a viable tradition of landscape in which specific, usually gentler effects of lighting and atmosphere, such as dawn and early dusk, gave their canvases a tranquil dignity which soon became a hallmark of this romantic trend. Camille Corot, who became one of the internationally popular artists of this general movement, did not actually belong to the Barbizon group, but he knew and encouraged its generally unrecognized members.

Rousseau's *Under the Birches, Evening* (Fig. 10) indicates the firm order which lay beneath the romantic gentleness of the style of most of the Barbizonists. Rousseau had, in fact, studied under the neoclassicist Lethière; and the organization of *Under the Birches* is closer to Davidian firmness than to the restlessness of Delacroix and

Figure 10. Théodore Rousseau. *Under the Birches, Evening,* c. 1842. 16⅝ × 25⅜″. (The Toledo Museum of Art, Toledo, Ohio. Gift of Arthur J. Secor, 1933.)

Figure 11. Jean-Baptiste Camille Corot. *Forest of Fontainebleau,* c. 1830. 69 × 95½". (National Gallery of Art, Washington, D. C. Chester Dale Collection.)

other romantic figure-painters. Yet in spite of the fine quality of this and similar canvases by the Barbizon painters, it was after midcentury before these men won official success at the Salon.

Charles Daubigny (1817–1878) was finally made a member of the Salon jury and in 1868 helped to admit the controversial impressionist canvases of Manet, Monet, Renoir, and others. Daubigny's works of the late 1850s with their special attention to lighting effects and reflections actually anticipated certain aspects of impressionism.

Jean-Baptiste Camille Corot (1796–1875), unlike his friends at Barbizon, was inspired by French and Italian neoclassical landscape; but his out-of-door studies of the Italian countryside and its villages confirmed his early style, upon which he imposed a peculiarly French discipline of structure. His water colors and oils of Italian ruins and houses were later admired by the postimpressionist Cézanne and by the early cubists of the twentieth century.

Around 1830 Corot developed a more sweeping but still ordered method shown in his *Forest of Fontainebleau* (Fig. 11). Its underlying rhythms of broadly patterned lights and darks are subtly complemented by tiny accents. Corot's canvases, like those of the Barbizonists, are usually conceived in terms of tonal effects rather than pure color. His late landscapes became increasingly hazy and somewhat less resolute in composition. It was only after his death that his excellent figure paintings became widely known.

French romantic landscape art was a viable tradition, stimulating the impressionists and later painters; but it suffers in effect from being too massively represented in a majority of museums. Scores of these canvases, whose tonalities and subjects are broadly similar, can become tiresome if presented together in a gallery, while a very few of them interspersed among paintings of a quite different and more vivid style can be enchanting.

English landscape art provides a long and rich tradition. It embraces some of the most inventive of British art, and it influenced Delacroix and other French romantics as well as the impressionists. Conversely, it was evidently Joseph Vernet of France who persuaded Richard Wilson (1714–1782), a pioneer of British landscape, to give up portraiture and turn to the other art.

Thomas Gainsborough (1727–1788), one of England's most distinguished portrait painters, worked sensitively in landscape. Alexander Cozzens, another predecessor of the British nineteenth-century romantics, discovered a curiously abstract-looking landscape method based on crumpled paper and ink blots reminiscent of psychological tests of recent times. Richard Bonington (1801–1828) was brought up in Calais and personally knew Delacroix and other Parisian artists, who admired his clear, informal but dignified water colors. The English tradition was climaxed by the gifted nineteenth-century romantics John Constable (1776–1837) and Joseph Mallord William Turner (1775–1851).

Constable, whose *The Hay Wain* and other works greatly stimulated Delacroix at the 1824 Salon, influenced both French and American landscape style without leaving England. Actually it was this artist's exciting, broken pigmentation and refreshing sweep of irregular yet orderly form, not his color as such, which so affected the Frenchmen. Constable's *Salisbury Cathedral* (Fig. 12) has that quality so delightfully characteristic of his mature style, the conjoinment of spontaneity and completeness.

Comparisons between Constable and Turner are likely to be invidious. Each of these major British artists contributed not only to the romantic landscape movement but to the broader tradition of modern art. We are often told of Constable's critical remark that his contemporary painted in tinted steam; but he also remarked that one of Turner's canal scenes was a complete work of genius. The nominal subject of Turner's *The Slave Ship* (Fig. 13), like the titles of most

Figure 12. John Constable. *Salisbury Cathedral*, c. 1827. (Reproduced by courtesy of the Trustees, The National Gallery, London.)

Figure 13. Joseph Mallord William Turner. *The Slave Ship*, 1839. 35¾ × 48″. (Courtesy, Museum of Fine Arts, Boston.)

of his works after about 1830, is so obscurely embedded in the astonishingly modern handling of the canvas that we must take effort to identify its particulars. His late style has, in fact, sometimes been compared with twentieth-century action painting; but, curiously, the fundamental subjects of action painting, its shapes, colors, and linear motifs, are much more readily identifiable.

The Slave Ship is topically based upon the bestial action of a trader's captain who cast overboard the still-living as well as the dead victims of a plague. It is interesting to compare Turner's treatment of a powerfully dramatic maritime theme with that of Géricault in the *Raft of the Medusa*. The French romantic, for all his tempestuousness, retains a certain rationale of expressiveness which does not altogether lose integration of style with content. Turner's swirling, almost expressionistic loosening of emotion and technique make of his subject the catalyst of a fantastic, visionary epic. In Turner's landscapes and maritime scenes, remarkable for their shimmering luminosity as well as their great intensity, we see the most modern of romantic attitudes toward the relative significance of form and theme.

The neoclassical and romantic traditions outside of France, Spain and England were definitive in the United States and Germany. Italy by the mid-eighteenth-century had yielded to France much of its formerly great international prestige, although its sculptors, as we shall presently see, were influential during the nineteenth century.

Benjamin West (1738–1820) was the first American painter to be widely acclaimed in Europe. Succeeding Sir Joshua Reynolds as president of the Royal Academy in London, West was responsible for the neoclassical training of a generation of younger Americans who studied in England. Some of West's historical canvases compare very favorably with French counterparts. Among the several Americans who trained in England, France, or Italy were John Vanderlyn, strongly Davidian in manner; Washington Allston, at first neoclassical but later strongly romantic (he is sometimes called a "visionary"); Gilbert Stuart, an especially brilliant portraitist who studied with West; and other artists whose Americanism is chiefly one involving American subject matter, for their various styles are solidly European. Thomas Cole of the Hudson River landscape group; Caleb Bingham, who appealingly depicted frontier scenes; and George Inness, whose landscapes are tinged with an early impressionism, are also characteristic of their place and time. Those who seek an especially home-grown trend of art in early to mid-nineteenth-century America will surely find many European neoclassical and romantic obstacles in the path.

Romanticism in German music and literature overshadowed its counterpart in the visual arts. Johan Heinrich Tischbein and Philipp

Otto Runge were significant early romantics. A pietistic group known as the Nazarenes, including Frederic Overbeck, Philip Veit, Peter Cornelius, and Wilhelm Schadow, lived and practiced in Rome, formulating a curiously literary style based partly upon renaissance ideals and to some extent mixing neoclassicism with romanticism (the Nazarenes are indirectly related, both in style and in attitude, to the English Preraphaelite brotherhood founded at midcentury by the poet-painter Dante Gabriel Rossetti, who is referred to in Chapter 3). Gottlieb Schick, Caspar David Friedrich, and Anselm von Feuerbach belonged essentially to the German neoclassical tradition.

REALISM

The movement in French art known as realism arose at midcentury as a challenge to the complacency and inversion of the Salon. It is to be noted that the public and the press (with certain notable exceptions) were as exercised by an art of specific naturalism as they would be during the twentieth century by such avant-garde manifestations as fauvism and cubism. Parisians had not strenuously reacted against most neoclassical and romantic art so long as it did not present distasteful subject matter; but the new realism of Jean François Millet and Gustave Courbet was more unsparingly detailed than that of the older movements and it also invoked subjects from everyday life, including peasants and their activities, ill-clad villagers, and intriguingly intimate girls on the banks of the Seine.

Millet (1814–1875) left the Barbizon association because he thought its program of idyllic landscapes was devoid of concern for man's struggle within nature. Although he denied that his solidly painted men and women of the soil, such as the couple in *The Angelus* (Fig. 14), were intended to reflect the radicalism of midcentury political theory and intellectual empathy with the worker, the middle-class public of Paris found, in the majesty of their lack of genuine sophistication about art, an objectionable crudeness in these sculpturesque figures and the raw earth beneath them. It is ironic that later critics found Millet's peasants not convincingly stained and rumpled. In any case, it is hard for late-twentieth-century eyes to objectively appreciate this artist's very respectable talents as an organizer of space and lighting; his *Man with the Hoe, The Gleaners, The Angelus,* and similar canvases were lithographically reproduced and hung in homes and schoolrooms throughout Europe and the United States before the end of the century, and overfamiliarity has deterred their appreciation.

Honoré Daumier (1808–1879) was also deeply sympathetic with workers and more especially with displaced or politically threatened

Figure 14. Jean François Millet. *The Angelus, 1859.* 21¾ × 26".
(The Louvre, Paris.)

people; but his vibrant, restless style, which combines one of the boldest of nineteenth century linear expressions with forceful dark-and-light modeling, is closer to the modern tradition than is Millet's art. But Daumier, exhausted during much of his life by the daily strain of creating satirical, political cartoons for the Parisian journals *La Caricature* and *La Charivari*, did not even have a one-man exhibition until friends arranged one a year before his death. He was by then almost totally blind from his graphic work, especially the technical process of plate-making for more than four thousand of the newspaper illustrations.

Daumier somehow managed to paint scores of canvases whose subjects and whose warmth of expressiveness appeal to our sense of humanity—political refugees on the march, interpretations of Cervantes' *Don Quixote*, washerwomen and their weary children, and occupants of overcrowded third-class carriages. But he never overburdened these themes with sentiment; he was a natural democrat with profound empathy for his subjects. *The Uprising* (Fig. 15) is one of his most stirring paintings, a work in which his probing, rapid line joins powerful brushwork and modeling to create a surging drama of revolt. Daumier achieves, with utmost economy of technical means, the essence of a collective force on the march, but a mass within which the identity of individuals is retained.

The controversial Gustave Courbet (1819–1877) is a major artist, the outstanding champion of realism and modern independence of spirit. At the time Courbet became an artist instead of studying law as his father preferred, it was becoming a moral decision-making problem as well as a professional matter to choose art as a means of livelihood. Courbet, like other young men in France at midcentury, was becoming aware that the Institute and its Salon were a block to independence and originality, that to defy it or to attempt to circumvent it usually led to obscurity or worse. Thus many young artists identified themselves with antiauthoritarianism in general. Courbet's career was,

Figure 15. Honoré Daumier. *The Uprising,* c. 1860(?). 24½ × 44½". (The Phillips Collection, Washington, D. C.)

in fact, sprinkled with controversies between him and any systematic form of authority. It was his good fortune that one of his canvases was exhibited at the liberal Salon of 1848, when, for a change, a liberating rather than a restrictive jury chose the entries. This early acceptance entitled Courbet to be represented in following official exhibitions.

It surprises many persons to know that remarkably few major artists have avowedly set out to realistically paint exactly what appeared before them; Caravaggio, a natural antecedent of Courbet, was one of them. By way of contrast, many great renaissance painters, Raphael for example, mentioned aesthetic principles which involved the creation of ideal types from a complex of ideal parts. Courbet desired to closely follow models of everyday life; but, like Caravaggio, he did much more than that. His most lucidly realistic works also reveal a masterful command of composition and selective lighting, as might be expected of one who searchingly studied such great masters as Giorgione, Velazquez, Rembrandt, Hals, as well as Caravaggio. Courbet also admired the vigor of Géricault and Delacroix, although he disapproved their romantic choice of literary subjects. There were also certain primitivizing elements in Courbet's style and imagery.[5]

Courbet's *A Burial at Ornans* (Fig. 16) synthesizes many aspects of his style and attitude. The huge painting at first appears to be randomly structured, like an accumulation of realistic notes. Actually it is firm in its undulating, horizontal pattern, whose somber lines echo in the distant cliffs. There are persuasive optical tensions between

Figure 16. Gustave Courbet. *A Burial at Ornans*, 1849. 10' 3" × 21' 9". (The Louvre, Paris.)

the sharp light tones in the clothing at the lower left and the scattered light notes of the dog and garments to the right and center. Courbet has also in psychological sweep further unified the composition by spanning in the figures all ages of man and, as signified by the distinctive dress of certain of the participants, has referred to specific phases of recent French history. It is ironic that the deceased hero of this plain but monumental drama is invisible.

Courbet's great independence of spirit was asserted in 1855 and again in 1867 when, refused the honor of exhibiting in the official galleries at the international expositions in Paris, he set up private booths nearby. The impressionists, postimpressionists, and the early twentieth century *fauves* would follow this astonishing precedent.

In spite of the public and journalistic hostility to Courbet, a few critics, notably Champfleury and Castagnary, acclaimed his originality and strength. Courbet was famous as well as controversial and was offered the Legion of Honor; but he declined it because he did not respect the existing administration in France.

Courbet was imprisoned for his part in the 1871 uprising, and spent the last four years of his life as a self-exile in Switzerland.

FOOTNOTES

[1] For a sympathetic evaluation, see Walter Pach's "The Heritage of Jacques Louis David" (*Gazette des Beaux-Arts*, XLV: 103-112, 1955).

[2] See the excellent study by Andrew C. Ritchie, "The Evolution of Ingres' Portrait of the Comtesse d'Haussonville" (*Art Bulletin* XXII: 119-126, 1940).

[3] This problem is effectively discussed by Geraldine Pelles in *Art, Artists, and Society* (Englewood Cliffs, N.J.: Prentice-Hall, Inc., 1963, pp. 9-14; 22-25).

[4] See Margaret Miller's "Géricault's Paintings of the Insane" (*Journal of the Warburg and Courtauld Institutes* XIV: 151-163, 1940-1941).

[5] See the notable study by Meyer Schapiro, "Courbet and Popular Imagery, An Essay on Realism and Naiveté" (*Journal of the Warburg and Courtauld Institutes* IV: 164-191, 1940-1941).

2

Manet to Renoir:
IMPRESSIONISM

The first independently arranged impressionist exhibition opened in the studio of the Parisian photographer Nadar in April, 1874. Few of the hundreds of startled visitors of the next few weeks could have traced the relationship of the refreshing, spontaneously brushed color and unmodeled form of the new pictures to the realistic tradition of the 1850s and 1860s, the atmospheric nature paintings of the Barbizonists, and the romantic verve of Gros, Géricault, and Delacroix.

Edouard Manet (1832–1883) was the artist whose style linked those recent traditions with the *nouvelle peinture* of Monet, Degas, Pissarro, Bazille, Cézanne, Sisley, Boudin, and other impressionists who until 1874 were known to their few admirers as the Batignolles group. The street of that name provided the Café Guerbois, at which, from about 1866, Manet led discussions between those artists and the critics Zola, Astruc, Duret, and Duranty. These conversations, which once grew so heated as to provoke the challenge to a duel, typically concerned the formal problems of lighting and atmospheric effects, color, the value of the Japanese print, and modern aspects of older art. The talk sometimes drifted to the hostility of Salon juries toward Courbet, a hero to Manet and certain others of the company, and toward themselves.

Manet's background included a well-to-do, cultivated family with genteel tastes and education. However, it was as if circumstances combined to make a revolutionary of him when his artistic goals were less aggressive. He studied for six argumentative years with the academician Couture, then underwent the influence of Dutch and Spanish masters. The Salon accepted two of his canvases in 1861.

In 1863, however, Manet's *Luncheon on the Grass* aroused public and academic anger, largely because of its allegedly ignoble subject, two fully and smartly attired young men in a wooded setting with two undressed females. The composition of this work was actually based upon a painting by Raphael as transcribed in an engraving by Raimondi. The *Luncheon* was included in a collection of works relegated to the *Salon des Refusés,* an unprecedented concession by the emperor Napoleon III to the protests of many artists who had by 1863 become vehement over repeated refusals by the academic juries.

Manet's *Olympia* (Fig. 17) was equally upsetting to visitors at the 1865 exhibition. This singularly bold nude study relates to both older and modern art. One traditional prototype is Titian's *Venus of Urbino* of 1535, whose sensuality certainly exceeds that of Manet's picture; but the artist also felt the influence of Courbet, whom he deeply admired, and Delacroix. His astonishingly disciplined but striking use of only one major light pattern against two dark ones, all three of them subtly marked by accents of middle tones, anticipates the flatly conceived, daring patterns of much postimpressionist and early twentieth century fauvist and expressionist art. *Olympia's* audacity of pose and crisp, unmodeled form outraged the moral and aesthetic sensibility of most spectators; but the canvas won for Manet the enthusiasm of the future Batignolles circle of painters and critics. The measure of his brilliantly handled, silvery grays and subtle-to-sharp contrasts of tone

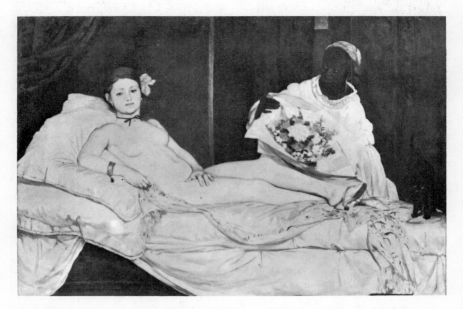

Figure 17. Edouard Manet. *Olympia,* 1863. 51¼ × 74¾″. (The Louvre, Paris.)

inspired these men. Although Manet never became an impressionist in the manner of Renoir and Monet, with their enchanting, vividly colored essays in reflected light and atmospheric nuances, he was indispensable to the development of impressionism.

Manet, determined in his genteel manner to win his conflicts with the academy *ad hoc,* refrained from exhibiting with his colleagues at the first impressionist show of 1874. His last major painting, however, is enough to identify him not only as an impressionist but as one of the masters of that style. *The Bar at the Folies Bergère* (Fig. 18) is a landmark, remarkable for its shimmering touch, its tinkling cluster of bright colors spanning the horizontal of grays and blacks and whites. This canvas firmly synthesizes impressionism with older painting. It is not merely a brilliant technical exercise, for the handsomely dressed young woman behind the bar is human in her curious melancholy. This vivacious work is a greater testimonial to Manet's achievement than were the Salon medal and the Legion of Honor, which he received a year before his death.

Figure 18. Edouard Manet. *The Bar at the Folies Bergère,* 1882. 37½ × 51". (Courtauld Institute Galleries, London.)

The history of impressionism, which greatly accelerated the stream of modern art, may be divided into three main phases: the formative, or early, from the *Salon des Refusés* of 1863 through 1873, during which Courbet's realist legacy, the Barbizon paintings, and Manet's personality are distinctive; the central, from the first group exhibition of 1874 until its eighth and last in 1886 and the advent of neoimpressionism; and the third, or late, from 1886 until the mid-1920s and the death of Monet, who, with Renoir, took the style beyond its proper and viable limits, for which about 1890 might be the reasonable mark.

Claude Monet (1840–1926) was a leader of impressionist innovation, and his paintings from about 1870 until 1890 include many scintillating documents of the movement. Like Manet, he was trained by an academician (in Monet's case, Charles Gleyre, whose studio housed other impressionists-to-be). His stronger influences, however, came from Eugène Boudin (1824–1898) and the Dutch-born Johan Jongkind (1819–1891), both of whom urged him to paint out of doors from nature and to not depend upon studio effects. Corot was another source.

The River (Fig. 19) reveals much of both Monet's style and of pre-1874 impressionist tendencies in general. While the *plein air,* or out-of-doors, aspect of impressionism has been overstressed, it is relevant that Monet and most of his associates chose themes whose lack of literary values or sentimentality enabled them to exploit their feelings and theories about color and light. *The River* is decidedly pleasant in content; the woman is a spectator of nature much as we are spectators of the painting. The artist's easy brushwork and relaxed colors and lighting are parallel with the woman's purely aesthetic role in the work. Typically impressionist in composition, the picture is almost random in its placement of forms and suggests unhurried, though spontaneous, execution.

The impressionists were excited not only by the peculiarly direct effects of outdoor sunlight, fog, and snow but also by the phenomena of interior lighting. An unusually complex problem is beautifully treated by Monet in his *Old St. Lazare Station, Paris* (Fig. 20), in which he observes the alliance of distant exterior light, the translucent glow from the glassed canopy above the locomotives, and the steam and smoke of the engines. This subject contains industrial forms which Monet only indirectly notes as he concentrates on the myriad touches which suggest the effects of machine-produced vapors.

It was Monet's *Impression: Sunrise,* a brightly colored, patchily textured canvas shown at the 1874 exhibition, that caused the reviewer Louis Leroy of *La Charivari* to cynically label the show as impressionist.

Figure 19. Claude Monet. *The River,* 1868. 31⅞ × 39½".
(Courtesy of The Art Institute of Chicago. Potter Palmer Collection.)

Monet and Camille Pissarro were among the most consistent of impressionists in their use of deliberately divided or broken hues to yield optical mixtures or blends, to modify or heighten the intensity of specific colors. Adjacent touches of green and red might produce an "optical gray," but, slightly separated, they might intensify one another. Red and yellow in separate patches would produce, according to theory, a more brilliant orange than the one given by mixing those colors on the palette. The impressionists more often painted outdoor scenes during the middle hours of the day than at dawn or dusk, the stages favored by the Barbizon landscapists. Monet created a series of canvases showing the changing tones of cathedral façades, haystacks, and other forms according to the movement of the sun or under specific conditions of haze.

Edgar Degas (1834-1917) was, like Manet, well-to-do and cosmopolitan in background. A strongly independent impressionist, he had little use for the optical phenomena of light and color as such,

Figure 20. Claude Monet. *Old St. Lazare Station, Paris,* 1877. (Courtesy of The Art Institute of Chicago. Mr. and Mrs. Martin A. Ryerson Collection.)

particularly in outdoor or *plein air* painting. His subject world was the café interior or terrace, the boulevards, the shops, the theater; and it was the mobility of the human figure in public or private gesture that captured him. Degas studied with Louis Lamothe, an Ingres product, and briefly attended the Ecole des Beaux Arts. He withdrew in order to study the old masters in Italy and at the Louvre. Draftsmanship—not the severe line of the academicians but a deft, rapid drawing—was always present in Degas' art. He delighted in stopping figures in space as they were in a complex, usually informal stage of movement.

Around 1882 Degas' themes became increasingly intimate and included women bathing, combing their hair, and shopping. *The Millinery Shop* (Fig. 21) is a subject purposely selected for its commonplaceness, the antithesis of the classical ideal of the noble subject. Degas' utility of this everyday motif, however, is unlike that of Millet or Courbet, who would have been interested in the humanity of the sitter. To Degas, the woman was no more and no less important as a pictorial

Figure 21. Edgar Degas. *The Millinery Shop,* c. 1885. 39⅛ × 43⅜″. (Courtesy of The Art Institute of Chicago. Mr. and Mrs. Lewis L. Coburn Memorial Collection.)

unit than the nearby unworn bonnets or the diagonal of the table; she serves as one element in the total design.

Degas appears to have been cogently instructed (as distinguished from stimulated or intrigued) by the Japanese print, although the effect was one of confirmation of his own inventiveness rather than direct influence.

Camille Pissarro (1830–1903) was the oldest of the impressionists. He had twice been accepted by the Salon before 1863, when he joined Manet, Cézanne, Whistler and others in the *Salon des Refusés.* He thereafter pursued his impressionist convictions, enduring decades of inadequate income and comparatively slight recognition. Pissarro was orthodox in his study of color and light, but he chose somewhat earthier subjects than did his colleagues, preferring the open countryside and

village streets. Unable to encourage younger artists financially, Pissarro
was respected by Cézanne, Van Gogh, and Gauguin for his warm
counsel. It was his insistence which won admission of Seurat and
Signac, the neoimpressionists, to the final impressionist exhibition.

Berthe Morisot (1841–1895) was a gifted woman painter who
had been recognized by the Salon in 1867 but who chose to join the
impressionists. A descendant of the rococo master Fragonard, she married Eugène Manet, brother of the impressionist painter. Morisot's un-
self-consciously feminine aesthetic was at first inspired by Corot, then
by Manet and Degas.

Alfred Sisley (1839–1899), born in Paris of British parents, was
unexcelled by any of his French colleagues in the painting of snowy
landscapes. His was a singularly pure kind of impressionism. Frédéric
Bazille (1841–1870) was killed during the Franco-Prussian war before
his style had fully matured. Certain of his small output of canvases
anticipate, in their brightness and touch, a mild postimpressionism.

Pierre Auguste Renoir (1841–1919) was a master of the impressionist style. After leaving a commercial decorating job and studying
with Gleyre, he had works accepted by the 1864 and 1865 Salons. He
met the future impressionists as students at Gleyre's atelier, and his
early development more or less paralleled that of Monet.

Renoir's sparkling, rich color and sensuous brushwork are central
to the growth of impressionism. He was enraptured by the magic
of reflected light and its transformation of local colors. However, Renoir
always remembered the great art of the museums and the humanity
of his figural subjects to a greater degree than did his friend Monet.
In the latter respect he was closer to Pissarro, although his technique
was more luminous.

Renoir's *The Luncheon of the Boating Party* (Fig. 22) is a monument of impressionism. Its appealing and characteristic theme, shimmering tonal passages and accents of pure color, and vibrant touch
are enchanting signs of Renoir's full development in the early 1880s.
Every zone of the canvas is vivacious and refreshing.

Renoir between 1883 and 1889 abandoned his fully impressionist
manner for one of severe drawing and restrained color, seeking a
new clarity of silhouette and monumentality of form. After 1900 his
nude compositions acquired an increasingly reddish tonality and soft
brushwork. He struggled valiantly against the crippling effects of
arthritis during his last fifteen years.

Two American artists, Mary Cassatt (1845–1926) and James Abbott
McNeill Whistler (1834–1903), were significant to the growth of
impressionism. It is one of the paradoxes of American art history and

Figure 22. Pierre Auguste Renoir. *The Luncheon of the Boating Party*, 1881. 51 × 68". (The Phillips Collection, Washington, D. C.)

criticism that a generation of early nineteenth-century painters had preceded Cassatt and Whistler in building their styles on European sources but are still unblushingly identified as distinctly American, whereas those two impressionists, following the precedent, neglected the detail of returning permanently to the United States and are called expatriates or self-exiles. This is singularly unfortunate, because Whistler and Cassatt represent their country's art with unexcelled distinction. Whistler was the last American to win first prize at the celebrated Venice Bieniale until it was awarded to the abstract painter Mark Tobey in 1958.

Mary Cassatt first studied at the Pennsylvania Academy of Fine Arts, then in Paris, where she joined the impressionists. Like her French coeval, Berthe Morisot, she was distinctly feminine in style; and she was at least as excellent a painter as Morisot.

Whistler was not a product of impressionism but one of its early, distinguished innovators. His statements about the priority of the formal elements of design and color over subject, made during the trial of his lawsuit against the English critic Ruskin in 1877, predate

the more widely known protoabstract statements of Gauguin and the
published theories of Denis and Sérusier. On the other hand, it is
specious to call Whistler a protoabstract painter because of the obscurity
of subject in such delightful compositions as his *Nocturne in Black and
Gold: The Falling Rocket* (Fig. 23). This and similarly exciting,
abstract-looking canvases of the 1870s simply denote Whistler's remarkably advanced variant of impressionism. To those who know

Figure 23. James Abbott Mc-
Neill Whistler. *Nocturne in
Black and Gold: The Falling
Rocket,* c. 1874. 23¾ ×
18⅜". (Courtesy of The Detroit Institute of Arts, Detroit.)

pyrotechnical displays as well as history of modern art, the *Nocturne in
Black and Gold: The Falling Rocket,* looks remarkably like an ex-
plosion of fireworks partly reflected in water, which is exactly what
Whistler was painting.

3

Postimpressionism:
NEOIMPRESSIONISM TO *ART NOUVEAU*

The two decades between 1884 and 1903 produced several developments which strongly accelerated the tradition of modern art. The neoimpressionist style, which soon replaced impressionism as the *nouvelle peinture,* appeared in Georges Seurat's systematically dotted canvases of 1886 in the final impressionist group show. The year 1903 was to witness the founding of the *Salon d'Automne,* which soon afterward presented the controversial art of the *fauves.* During the twenty-year interval, avant-garde associations formed in Brussels, Munich, Vienna, Berlin, and London as well as in Paris. Artists of independent vision everywhere were now determined to further the precedent of the independent, extraofficial exhibitions and resistance to academic controls which had been set by the impressionists and anticipated by Courbet's intransigeance.

SEURAT AND THE *INDÉPENDANTS*

The displacement of impressionism as the major group style of the 1870s and 1880s, the advent of neoimpressionism (also called *pointillisme*), and the growth of the trends loosely and collectively called postimpressionism, afford a complex history. Certain impressionists, Renoir and Pissarro among them, felt soon after 1880 that they had taken the style to its correct limits. Paul Gauguin and Paul Cézanne, among others, had never fully subscribed to impressionist theories and now began to seek independent values. Van Gogh, who became familiar with impressionist leaders only as late as 1886, the year of their final exhibition, soon withdrew to Arles to seek an expressive method of his own. Seurat, Paul Signac, Henri-Edmond Cross, Dubois-Pillet, Angrand, and other neoimpressionists felt that impressionism, so extensively involved with factors of color and light, lacked scientific discipline.

It is inexact, however, to suppose that postimpressionism and its diversified styles were based upon a forthright reaction against impressionism.[1] The new artists were vigorous and determined to validate their ideas; but the impressionist legacy, especially its efforts to exploit the spot or patch of color as a structural element within the overall composition, was most relevant to the later trends.

Georges-Pierre Seurat (1859–1891) developed neoimpressionism during 1883 and 1884 and helped to found the *Société des Artistes Indépendants*, whose special exhibitions, in the manner of the impressionist shows, furthered the recognition of the new style. Although Seurat had exhibited a drawing at the official Salon of 1883, he and most of the Independents had more often been rejected than recognized. Even the once avant-garde impressionists objected to including Seurat's and Signac's canvases in their last show, and only Pissarro's sympathy effected their inclusion. The alert critic Felix Fénéon was one of Seurat's few advocates.

Seurat's celebrated *Sunday Afternoon on the Island of La Grande Jatte* (Fig. 24) is an outstanding monument of its style. It illustrates

Figure 24. Georges Seurat. *Sunday Afternoon on the Island of La Grande Jatte*, 1884-86. 81 × 120⅜". (Courtesy of The Art Institute of Chicago. Helen Birch Bartlett Memorial Collection.)

the young artist's urge to pring to painting a firm new order of composition as well as controlled but inventive color relationships. Although it was his friend Signac who wrote the definitive treatise on pointillist theory, Seurat referred in correspondence to the specific optical and emotional responses which he intended to stimulate by using horizontal rhythms in rising sequence, as well as to his intended effects of minute, confetti-like dots of pure colors and tones. The scientific aspect of Seurat's method is often overstressed; the luminosity and structural ingenuity of his half-dozen finished masterpieces are based upon systems which were essential to his particular purposes,[2] just as the more spontaneous touch and color of the impressionists were formulated to meet other needs. Mathematical and optical design and refinements were practiced by the fifth century Greeks and many renaissance artists, and Seurat by no means discovered scientific applications to the fine arts. His and Signac's study of the theories of Chevreul, Helmholtz, O. N. Rood, and others did not result in an exact extension of their principles onto canvas. It is true, however, that the neoimpressionists were remarkably systematic in their method of color and design. To be in the presence of Seurat's *La Grande Jatte* is to confront a great stylistic masterpiece. The artist had made literally hundreds of drawings and oil sketches for this huge canvas. Seurat, who had studied under an Ingres-trained neoclassicist and who deeply admired the solemn compositions of Puvis de Chavannes, felt that impressionism had come to be formless, and his significant contribution to the modern tradition is as much his revitalization of ordered composition as his discoveries of new luminosities of color.

After Seurat's death, at age thirty-two, the neoimpressionist style was continued by Signac (1863–1935) and Henri-Edmond Cross (1856–1910); but neither man amplified the great achievement of their colleague.

GAUGUIN; VAN GOGH; TOULOUSE-LAUTREC; CÉZANNE

Paul Gauguin (1848–1903) was thirty-five before he devoted his full energies to painting. Like his friend Van Gogh, he was impelled to communicate through art a strongly personal vision of which color and shape were the exteriorized, intense symbols. Benefiting from impressionism but outgrowing its perceptual methods, Gauguin searched for new conceptual values and emotional certainty in Brittany, overseas in Martinique, to Arles in southern France, where he and Van Gogh unfortunately broke off their friendship, and ultimately to Polynesia, where he died without realizing the power and significance of his post-impressionist art. He led the movements known as *synthetism* and *cloisonnism,* and for a time headed the Parisian symbolist poets and painters. In the most generalized sense, the common aim of these groups was independently to discover unique values of painting or literature and to transform them into deeply personal, metaphoric images, ostensibly recognizable in form but symbolic in intent.

The radiant color usually associated with Gauguin's late works done in Tahiti was actually even more vivid in his synthetist canvases of the 1880s, which he painted in Brittany partly under the emotional and visual stimulus of medieval carvings and primitive folk art, as in his *The Yellow Christ* (Fig. 25). Wayside shrines provided the blunt

Figure 25. Paul Gauguin. *The Yellow Christ,* 1889. 36¼ × 28⅞". (Albright-Knox Art Gallery, Buffalo, New York.)

imagery of this startling, powerfully colored and starkly designed painting whose style was soon to influence the German expressionists and French *fauves.*

Two Tahitian Women (Fig. 26), painted by Gauguin ten years later, shows the calmer but still radiantly colored manner of his last, poverty- and disease-ridden years in a primitive environment, whose

Figure 26. Paul Gauguin. *Two Tahitian Women*, 1899. 37 × 28½". (The Metropolitan Museum of Art. Gift of William Church Osborn, 1949.)

once inspiring freshness had been vitiated by European colonial rule. But Gauguin endured his privations long enough to create the late monuments of a postimpressionist style which greatly impelled early twentieth century artists.

Gauguin's one-time friend, Vincent Van Gogh (1853–1890), also experienced a tragic career, and he similarly left to recent modern art a brilliantly creative legacy. Failing as a salesman of fine arts for a renowned gallery and as a preacher among underpriviliged miners, Van Gogh turned to full-time practice of an art he had always wanted to express. He was largely self-taught through his almost reverent study of Rembrandt, Delacroix, Corot, and Courbet and his later influences by the impressionists and Puvis de Chavannes. Like Gauguin, Van Gogh longed to bring to painting an intensely personal symbolism conveyed through an independent mystique. Although Van Gogh's style was liberated by impressionist color and touch, he went beyond the perceptual character of that method and expressed a vibrantly intense communication with his subjects, at the same time founding a singularly effective power of hues and structure as in his *L'Arlésienne* (*Portrait of Mme Ginoux*) (Fig. 27) and *Mme Roulin and Her Baby* (Fig. 28).

Figure 27. Vincent Van Gogh. *L'Arlésienne (Portrait of Mme Ginoux)*, 1888. 36 × 29". (The Metropolitan Museum of Art. Bequest of Samuel A. Lewisohn, 1951.)

Figure 28. Vincent Van Gogh. *Mme Roulin and Her Baby.* 1888-89. (Collection of the Philadelphia Museum of Art.)

These exciting images, particularly the mother and child, are very close to twentieth-century expressionist art. His empathy with these two persons (Madame Roulin often posed for Van Gogh when he could not afford models) was so emotionally charged that his drawing of the child's forms becomes almost like the drawing by a child of another. It should be quickly added that Van Gogh, a direct and powerful draftsman, never lost his remarkably sensitive ability to organize compositions even during the period in his last two years when he suffered from a still incompletely diagnosed mental illness. His last, turbulent canvas, *Crows over the Wheatfield* (Fig. 29), is painted with great,

Figure 29. Vincent van Gogh. *Crows over the Wheatfield*, 1890. 20⅛ × 39¾". (Stedelijk Museum, Amsterdam.)

almost prophetic urgency; but its underlying pattern is resolute. A few days after completing this canvas he committed suicide.

Henri de Toulouse-Lautrec (1864–1901) is sometimes identified with the impressionist rather than the postimpressionist movement. His style is in fact indicative of certain trends in each of those general tendencies, and his draftsmanship, distinguished and probing, was in part inspired by Degas. Descendant of an ancient French family, Lautrec suffered a childhood injury which shattered his legs and stunted his growth, leaving him dwarfish in appearance. He sought refuge, after studying art, in the demimonde atmosphere of Montmartre, making friends with Parisian outcasts, with whom he felt a strange empathy. His biting line and acid colors matured in the milieu of brothels, workers' cafés, and night cabarets which during the 1880s and 1890s provided lurid entertainment for well-to-do visitors from all over the world. *At the Moulin Rouge* (Fig. 30) belies Lautrec's early training with the academician Louis Bonnat. The artist paints his own grotesque figure in this work, contained within the silhouette of the tall man in the middle of the distant plane. Lautrec was an innovator in color lithography, especially in the poster medium; and his fluid shapes and lines show an affinity with the turn-of-the-century decorative style known as the *art nouveau.*

Most authorities agree that Paul Cézanne (1839–1906) is the profoundest source of modern painting. His father, like Courbet's, wanted the son to study law, not art. Settling in Paris after leaving Aix-en-Provençe in southern France, Cézanne failed his entrance examinations at the Ecole des Beaux-Arts but doggedly studied at the Académie Suisse, where there was little formal instruction.

Figure 30. Henri de Toulouse-Lautrec. *At the Moulin Rouge,* 1892. 48⅜ × 55¼". (Courtesy of The Art Institute of Chicago. Helen Birch Bartlett Memorial Collection.)

   This giant of postimpressionism experienced a lifetime of incredible neglect, although he exhibited with the impressionists and had a small partisan following. His first significant attention was a large one-man show given by the dealer Ambroise Vollard in 1895. Meanwhile, the Salon juries had repeatedly refused his paintings, accepting only one, on the personal plea of a juror, during twenty years.

   Cézanne, like his contemporaries Van Gogh and Gauguin, owed much to impressionism; but he, too, sought to go beyond its principles, to develop an enduring art like that of the museums, as he put it. He withdrew from Paris to the seclusion of Aix, where, after agonizing searching, he formulated a new way of painting.

   In the masterful still-lifes, figure compositions, and landscapes from the late 1880s until his death, in 1906 (Figs. 31, 32, 33), Cézanne resolved a troublesome paradox of painting, a problem which he may also have been the first fully to recognize. Respecting the two-dimensional character of the picture-plane, he was able to also achieve

Figure 31. Paul Cézanne. *Still Life with Apples*, 1890-1900. 27 × 36½". (Collection, The Museum of Modern Art, New York. Lillie P. Bliss Collection.)

Figure 32. Paul Cézanne. *The Large Bathers,* 1898-1905. 82 × 99".
(Philadelphia Museum of Art. W. P. Wilstach Collection.)

solidity and spatial depth. His method, which was exerted in a
patchwork of overlapping, translucent strokes, related each shape,
color, and plane to the different zones of the composition—a revolutionary and viable system.

Cézanne's immediate heirs were the early cubists; but all major
twentieth-century trends have been instructed by his discovery.

THE *NABIS, JUGENDSTIL,* AND ART NOUVEAU

Other special styles and movements, some of them more or less
mystic or otherwise esoteric, arose between 1890 and 1900 in France,
Belgium, England, Germany, Austria, and America. The synthetists
and symbolists, already mentioned in connection with Gauguin, included the poet Stèphane Mallarmé; the painter and lithographer

Figure 33. Paul Cézanne. *Mont Sainte Victoire,* 1904-06. (Philadelphia Museum of Art. George W. Elkins Collection.)

Odilon Redon (1840–1916) (Fig. 34), a precursor of the recent surrealists; and Paul Sérusier (1863–1927) and Maurice Denis (1870–1943), painters and theorists. Redon also led the *Rose-Croix* circle, whose membership overlapped with that of the symbolists, the *nabis,* and the *intimistes.* The composers Satie and Debussy, the poets Verlaine, Rimbaud, and Pierre Louÿs, and the painters Ferdinand Hodler (Swiss), Edvard Munch (Norwegian), and James Ensor (Belgian) were directly or indirectly in touch with one or more of those groups. The *nabis* (from the Hebrew word, "prophet") and intimists numbered Edouard Vuillard, Pierre Bonnard, Felix Vallotton, and several others. James McNeill Whistler and the Englishman Aubrey Beardsley also knew various of these men.

If the reader is baffled by this amassment of names—and others might well have been added—he should not be discouraged. Excellent studies have been made of turn-of-the-century art and its personalities; but none has fully linked these with the international mode of decoration and design known in France and Belgium as *art nouveau,* in Germany as *Jugendstil,* in Vienna as *Sezessionstil,* and *modernismo* in Spain.

Art nouveau, as this movement is almost universally called today, had important roots in England, including William Morris's arts and crafts movement which had begun in the 1850s and was supported by the critic John Ruskin; and there are connections, too, with the Pre-raphaelite Brotherhood of Dante Gabriel Rossetti, John Everett Millais, William Holman Hunt, Thomas Woolner, Frederic George Stephens, and others, founded in 1848. The romantic, visionary William Blake (1757–1827) is also regarded by certain historians as an antecedent of the modern movement, as *art nouveau's* British parallel was called. Other sources of this bizarre style were Japanese prints and popular furnishings, Minoan vase painting, and heraldic ornament from Egypt and Mesopotamia.

The *art nouveau* cluster of styles had both symbolic, romantic, and purely inventive characteristics which were typically synthesized in a sinuous, self-consciously ornate linearism, not unrelated to plant tendrils and the curved necks of swans. The arabesques of this curious, elaborate manner were prominent throughout Europe and in the United States in textiles, glassware (especially Tiffany's), book illustrations and

Figure 34. Odilon Redon. *The Cyclops,* c. 1900. 25 × 19⅞". (Rijksmuseum Kröller-Müller, Otterlo, Holland.)

typography, and furniture. The Belgian architects Victor Horta and Henry van de Velde practiced this style in certain monuments, as did the Spaniard Antoni Gaudí, and, in Great Britain, Charles Mackintosh, A. H. Mackmurdo, Charles Voysey, and others. It affected to some extent the work of several American architects.

Edvard Munch (1863–1944) of Norway, in his moody, curvilinear compositional rhythms, was related to *Jugendstil;* but in his somber canvases and woodcuts, these undulating lines become the carriers of deeper emotions, as in his *Puberty* (Fig. 35), whose conjoined technical and emotional impact stirred the German expressionists of 1905 and

Figure 35. Edvard Munch. *Puberty*, 1895. 59 × 43¾". (National Gallery, Oslo, Norway.)

later. In certain of Munch's works, these rising, sinking linear paths resemble the illustrations in children's geology books showing crustal movements of the earth.

The Belgian James Ensor (1860–1947), an exact contemporary of Munch, also influenced the twentieth-century expressionists. An eccentric recluse who spent most of his life in the same house in Belgium, Ensor, a precociously brilliant draftsman, grew increasingly hostile toward critics and artists alike (he referred to most groups of his colleagues as charlatans and impostors). His own mature style was considerably influenced by impressionism, which he disliked. His deliberately smeary, abused textures anticipate the surfaces of many recent abstract artists.

Ensor's huge canvas, *The Entry of Christ into Brussels in 1889* (Fig. 36), painted the previous year, is his diatribe against the babbling, insensitive multitude which would be callous even to the reappearance of Jesus. Partisan factions of the crowd, displaying their banners, and masked, deathlike faces which symbolize falseness, continue their prattling; while the image of Christ, although centralized, is almost indistinct.

Other European artists contributed to the remarkable variety of postimpressionist styles, including the Germans Hans von Marées (1837–1887), who influenced Max Beckmann and other modern expressionists, and Arnold Böcklin (1827–1901), whose melancholy allegories inspired De Chirico and the surrealists.

Mary Cassatt and James Whistler have been mentioned in relation to impressionism. Winslow Homer (1836–1910), Thomas Eakins (1844–1916) and John Singer Sargent (1856–1925) also contributed saliently to late nineteenth century art. Of these Americans, Eakins

Figure 36. James Ensor. *The Entry of Christ into Brussels in 1889,* 1888. 101½″ × 169½″. (Musée Royal des Beaux-Arts, Anvers, Belgium.)

Figure 37. Edouard Vuillard. *Interior at L'Etang-la-Ville*, 1893. 12½ × 14 5/16". (Smith College Museum of Art, Northampton, Massachusetts.)

practiced a specific but nonetheless independent realism. Both he and Homer visited France during their youth, and the influence of European styles upon their naturalism has not yet been fully evaluated. Sargent, a brilliant portrait painter who was to some extent influenced by impressionism, has suffered, like Whistler and Cassatt, for spending much of his career abroad; for some American critics still identify him with European art. Another important, independent artist in the United States was Albert Pinkham Ryder (1847-1917), a recluse, neglected by his contemporaries but admired by younger modern painters such as Marsden Hartley.

Edouard Vuillard (1868–1940) and Pierre Bonnard (1867-1947) were two French painters whose styles, although they obtained until nearly the center of the present century, belonged chronologically and formatively to the postimpressionist epoch. Both men admired

the impressionists and Toulouse-Lautrec but were little influenced by
Van Gogh and Cézanne. They represent a more genteel strain of postimpressionism, and the name of the movement with which they are
usually identified, intimism, indicates much of their aesthetic. Vuillard's
Interior at L'Etang la Ville (Fig. 37) and Bonnard's *Dining Room in
the Country* (Fig. 38) show their consummate, restrained brushwork
and design. Their colored posters in lithographic medium, many of them
done for *La Revue Blanche,* combine the *nabi* and intimist approach
with *art nouveau* fluidity of line and silhouette. The emotional drives
of Van Gogh and Cézanne were alien to them.

Figure 38. Pierre Bonnard. *Dining Room in the Country,* 1913. 63 ×
80". (The Minneapolis Institute of Arts. John R. Van Derlip Fund,
1954.)

FOOTNOTES

[1]This problem is thoughtfully discussed by Fritz Novotny in "The Reaction
Against Impressionism from the Artistic Point of View," in *Problems of the
Nineteenth and Twentieth Centuries* (Millard Meiss, ed.) (Princeton, N.J.: Princeton
University Press, 1963, pp. 93-103).

[2]See Meyer Schapiro, "New Light on Seurat" (*Art News,* LVII: 22 ff., 1958).

4

Some Nineteenth Century
Sculpture and Sculptors

Nineteenth century neoclassical and romantic sculpture by no means equalled the painting of those movements. There was no Jacques Louis David or Delacroix of third dimensional art, and it was not until late in the nineteenth century that genuinely original talents emerged. Meanwhile, scores of neoclassicists produced generally skillful but uninspiring nudes, portraits, and thousands of those solemn, public monuments of the heroes of war and peace which still loom upon the horizon and often impede the proper flow of traffic.

NEOCLASSICISM AND ECLECTICISM

Antonio Canova (1757–1822) was already celebrated in his native Italy when he became Napoleon's court sculptor in France. His portraits of the Emperor (Fig. 39) are technically skillful, and occasional small-scale studies like the *Kreugas* (Fig. 40) display a less formalized vigor. He also did nude figures in heroic scale of both Napoleon and his sister, Pauline Borghese, whom he portrayed as a reclining Venus.

Canova's neoclassicist prestige brought scores of European and American sculptors to France and Italy. Only his contemporary, the Norwegian Bertel Thorwaldsen (1768–1844), rivaled his position as a teacher of neoclassicism.

David d'Angers (Pierre-Jean David) and the Italian Lorenzo Bartolini sustained Canova's manner until midcentury without significantly personalizing it. A slightly younger generation, which included Giovanni Dupré, Vincenzo Vela, and Jean-Alexandre Falguière, created an efflorescence of the inexorable public statue.

François Rude infused the neoclassical style with a certain verve, drawing attention to heroic movement as in his *Departure of the Volunteers* of 1836 at the Arch of Triumph in Paris. Rude was influen-

Figure 39. Antonio Canova. *Bust of Napoleon.* Marble, H. 21¾". (Collection of the Philadelphia Museum of Art.)

Figure 40. Antonio Canova. *Kreugas,* 1806. Bronze, H. 25¼". (The University of Kansas Museum of Art.)

tial as a teacher, and his student Jean-Baptiste Carpeaux developed a notably graceful, mobile style with modulations of surface which opposed the steely polish of most neoclassical statues. His *Neapolitan Fisherboy* (Fig. 41) reveals an almost rococo vivacity and a complexity of movement in space. Carpeaux's celebrated *The Dance,* a cavorting circle of figures designed for the façade of the Paris Opera House, was protested by a public which distinguished between nudity, nakedness, and the state of undress.

Antoine-Louis Barye (1796–1875) also contributed a mild antidote to Italianate, neoclassical severity. An instructor of drawing at the Paris Museum of Natural History, he became one of the most universally popular sculptors of animals. His bronze *Tiger Devouring an Antelope* (Fig. 42) displays the robust movement which has been likened to romantic painting style; but its more exaggerated examples led the critic Gautier to unappreciatively call Barye the Michelangelo of the menagerie.

Figure 41. Jean-Baptiste Carpeaux. *Neapolitan Fisherboy,*
1861. Marble, H. 36¼".
(National Gallery of Art, Washington, D. C. Samuel H. Kress
Collection.)

Jules Dalou, who studied with Carpeaux, was widely influential,
especially in England, for combining certain elements of neoclassicism
and romanticism; and Jean Antonin Mercié, Emmanuel Frémiet, and
Henri Michel Antoine Chapu produced many public statues but contributed little to stylistic development.

An entire generation of American sculptors studied or practiced in
Rome or Florence during the first half of the nineteenth century (it
has been mentioned that American painters studied the neoclassical
style in Italy or in London during this period); and a younger contingent gravitated toward Paris and the Ecole des Beaux-Arts. Most of
these men became quite as technically proficient, and remained as
typically unoriginal, as their European coevals. Hiram Powers, Horatio
Greenough, Thomas Crawford, William Wetmore Story, and Randolph
Rogers studied in the general manner of Canova or Thorwaldsen.
Followers of the somewhat more romantic-eclectic method of the French

academies were Olin Levi Warner, Frederick W. MacMonnies, Paul Wayland Bartlett, George Gray Barnard, and the internationally reputable Daniel Chester French (1850–1931). Augustus Saint-Gaudens (1860–1936), who was born in Dublin, also belongs to this group, although he and French were especially sensitive in their adaptations of Ecole des Beaux-Arts style. Lorado Taft, another American favorite (1860–1936), is important for having written a history of his nation's sculpture.

The least eclectic of American sculptors during this period was the Boston physician and anatomist William Rimmer (1816–1879), who was self-taught in art.

England similarly produced its complement of Italian and Parisian-trained neoclassicists and academic-romanticists whose efforts in the main resembled those of their contemporaries everywhere. John Gibson, Francis Chantrey, and W. Calder Marshall were fully neoclassical; Alfred Stevens, George Frederick Watts, Sir William Hamo Thornycroft, E. Onslow Ford, and Charles Lawes-Wittewronge left proper and dignified public statuary somewhat less severe than the neoclassicists'. England lacked a Constable or Turner in sculpture as France lacked a David or Delacroix.

In Germany, a more personalized neoclassicism was developed by the sculptor and theoretician Adolf von Hildebrand (1847–1921),

Figure 42. Antoine Louis Barye. *Tiger Devouring an Antelope,* c. 1851. Bronze, L. 22½". (Philadelphia Museum of Art. W. P. Wilstach Collection.)

Figure 43. Adolf von Hildebrand. *The Net Carrier,* 1875.
Stone. (Bayerische Staatsge-
mäldesammlungen, Munich.)

whose *The Net Carrier* (Fig. 43) displays a sensitively adapted classical
influence not to be confused with typical academic practices of its
time. Max Klinger was an early admirer of Rodin's independent and
vigorous style and reacted against von Hildebrand's classicism. August
Gaul was celebrated in Germany for his animal sculptures much as
Barye was in France.

Constantin Meunier and Rik Wouters, Belgian realists, were strongly
independent in their art. Their compatriot Georges Minne (1866–1941)
combined realism with what may be called protoexpressionist distortion
and attenuation of form and pose. He was influential upon certain
German modern sculptors.

PAINTER-SCULPTORS

The first French artist to reject midcentury eclecticism was not
a sculptor, but the painter-lithographer Honoré Daumier. Of his fifty

Figure 44. Edgar Degas. *Grand Arabesque,* n.d. Bronze, H. 11⅜". (Los Angeles County Museum of Art. Mr. and Mrs. George Gard de Sylva Collection.)

to sixty known portraits, caricatures, and small figural groups in sculpture, nearly all were made as self-instruction for his painting and graphic work. These sculptures are refreshingly conceived and powerfully modeled, their surfaces broken and vigorous—an art much in advance of its time.

Another painter, Edgar Degas, also created a number of sculptures daring in mobility, like his canvases and pastels. His *Grand Arabesque* (Fig. 44) is characteristic in pose and in its spontaneous textures.

Auguste Renoir is still another nineteenth-century painter who may be called a sculptor, although almost none of his bronzes were modeled or completed by his own hands. Renoir, physically incapable of handling the medium because of arthritis by the time he seriously wanted to make sculpture, supervised an assistant who developed the models from drawings.

RODIN AND ROSSO

Auguste Rodin (1840–1917) was the first giant of sculpture in nineteenth-century France. His influence has been incalculably great, if controversial, throughout the world. Rodin was saliently independent. It is incorrect to identify him as an impressionist, for the irregularity of his surfaces resulted from an almost expressionistic vigor in which deliberate gougings and pressings of the fingers were emotionally as well as technically directed. Trained by academicians and by Barye (of whom he always spoke well), Rodin's true sources were Donatello, Michelangelo, and the Gothic carvers. These were translated, however, in a singularly liberated style. Three of Rodin's sculptures can suggest, though not fully exemplify, the range of his expressive power: *The Burghers of Calais, The Gates of Hell,* and *The Kiss* (Figs. 45, 46, 47).

Rodin did not hesitate to invoke heroic, literary themes; but these did not dominate his monumental handling of them, and he was repelled by most of the academic sculpture of his time, which was oppressively literary.[1] *The Gates of Hell,* which was unfinished when Rodin died, demonstrates how his intensely dramatic figures, inspired largely by Dante and Baudelaire, equal the highly expressive language of those poets.

Figure 45. Auguste Rodin. *The Burghers of Calais,* 1888. Bronze, 84 × 91". (Rodin Museum, Philadelphia. Courtesy Philadelphia Museum of Art.)

Figure 46. Auguste Rodin. *The Gates of Hell*, 1880-1917. Bronze, H. 18". (Rodin Museum, Philadelphia. Courtesy Philadelphia Museum of Art.)

Figure 47. Auguste Rodin. *The Kiss*, 1883. Marble copy of the original, executed by H. Gréber, signed A. Rodin, 72 × 44" at the base. (Courtesy Philadelphia Museum of Art.)

Figure 48. Medardo Rosso. *Conversation in a Garden*, 1893. Bronze.
(Galleria Nazionale d'Arte Moderna, Rome.)

Medardo Rosso (1858–1928) was Italy's most distinguished nine-teenth-century sculptor. His *Conversation in a Garden* (Fig. 48) shows the astonishing modernity of his rippling, half-melted forms, which are much closer to impressionist painting than Rodin's art (these two men admired one another). Rosso's style is surprisingly liberated; he deliberately smeared away sections of articulated form into passive areas so that other specific parts of a figure or group might receive greater emphasis. Unfortunately for the history of twentieth-century style, Rosso's wax and bronze art was scarcely known outside Italy until after 1900. He might well have become a chief source of recent sculpture.

FOOTNOTE

[1]See Albert E. Elsen's discussion of Rodin's themes in his *Rodin* (New York: Museum of Modern Art, 1963, especially pp. 35-47; 70-87).

The Twentieth Century:
FAUVISM TO EARLY ABSTRACT ART

The arts of the first fifteen years of the twentieth century were so viable that they anticipated all major trends which have followed. Fauvism, expressionism, cubism, futurism, dada, and abstraction, as these vigorous new styles were called, had in turn been implicit in the most fertile of postimpressionist tendencies.

Between 1900 and 1905, showings of the provocative works of Cézanne, Van Gogh, Gauguin, Seurat, Redon, Munch, and other late-nineteenth-century innovators were held in various major European cities. A new generation of artists who had seen little or none of this strong tradition enthusiastically responded to its stimulus and challenge. New groups, determined to place their own discoveries before the public, were formed. Official salons everywhere were as impervious as ever to artistic liberation; but the voices of protest grew stronger against academic inertia as insurgents in Berlin, Vienna, and Paris struggled for recognition by their governments. Older factions were split, new ones became adamant.

THE *FAUVES* AND THE *SALON D'AUTOMNE*

The Salon des Indépendants, founded in 1884 by Seurat and his associates, had continued into the early 1900s to show postimpressionist art which was still unacceptable to the Institute. A new force, however, wished to extend facilities to the most recent trends. Its leaders, especially Henri Matisse and Georges Rouault, overcame academic resistance and in 1903 founded the celebrated *Salon d'Automne*. These men not only desired an honorable outlet for their art; but they were also ideologically determined to revitalize French painting, overcoming the vitiated trends of the academy much as had the impressionists and the postimpressionists in their time.

Most of the younger avant-gardists in Paris had been studying during the 1890s under academicians who had not encouraged their looking at postimpressionism of a more vigorous kind than *nabi* and intimist harmonies. Now they were exhilarated by the recent exhibitions which disclosed the chromatic urgency of Van Gogh and Gauguin and the structural inventions of Cézanne; and they were beginning to unleash their energies in spontaneously brushed, vividly hued canvases.

The first massive showing of works by Matisse, Rouault, Georges Desvallières, Albert Marquet, Othon Friesz, Louis Valtat, Henri Manguin, Charles Camoin, Raoul Dufy, and Kees Van Dongen appeared in a room in the 1905 Salon d'Automne. The shocked, unprepared reviewer Louis Vauxcelles derisively called their gallery the *cage des fauves* (cage of the wild beasts), forgetting the unlucky precedent of Louis Leroy, who similarly dubbed impressionism, an art which had finally become popular in France. The fauvist exhibition was showered with public and journalistic insult; but it also won supporters. The Salon d'Automne itself soon became tolerated, then accepted, and finally institutionalized.

We might remind ourselves that young artists, beginning around the center of the nineteenth century, became aware that to follow their profession involved moral as well as professional decisions. To adhere to the orthodoxy of the academies in France, Germany, England, Austria, and elsewhere called for a certain compromise of conscience in many cases; for young painters and sculptors knew and to one or another degree admired their innovating contemporaries, and to choose the less adventuresome, more secure way of the academy became a significant problem.

Henri Matisse (1869–1954), leader of the *fauves,* was past thirty-five when he cast his lot with the new group, an age when most men hesitate to substantively change professional goals. Further, he had actually changed professions once before, leaving the beginning practice of law to study academic art. He had become a skilled copyist of old master paintings in the Louvre and might have had a steady career as a conventional painter. Thus his turn to the radical style of the day involved great commitment. It was Matisse's good fortune that his talents and energies won great prestige, and he later became one of the most influential artists of this century.

Matisse's fauvist works of 1905–1906, the greatest years of this movement, summarize the astonishingly liberating qualities of the art of the whole group. Pure vermilion, oranges, blues, greens, violets, yellows worked vividly in a rushing patchwork of inventive strokes.

Figure 49. Henri Matisse. *The Blue Window*, 1911. 51½ × 35⅝″. (Collection, The Museum of Modern Art, New York. Abby Aldrich Rockefeller Fund.)

Occasional linear arabesques helped to define free shapes. Space was usually flattened by color tensions which resulted from repetition of equally intense accents in distance as well as in foreground. The network of vigorous spots and dashes of pigment served as a reinforcement of the apparently random compositions.

Matisse was more cogently affected by Cézanne's structural methods than were most of his colleagues. He also briefly experimented with the dynamics of cubism, giving personal interpretation to its rhythmic repetitions of a design motif, as in the circular patterns of his *The Blue Window* (Fig. 49).

Between 1910 and about 1917 Matisse explored several methods of expression, strengthening color, line, texture, and spatial relations. His extensive knowledge not only of traditional art but Minoan and Islamic decoration, African tribal carvings, *art nouveau,* and other exotic forms, enriched his expressive powers. Many of his strongest works, such as *Studio, Quai St. Michel* (Fig. 50), date before 1920, after which his style became increasingly decorative, though still vigorous.

Figure 50. Henri Matisse. *Studio, Quai St. Michel*, 1916. 57½ × 45¾". (The Phillips Collection, Washington, D. C.)

Figure 51. André Derain. *Portrait of Henri Matisse*, 1905. 13 × 16". (Philadelphia Museum of Art. A. E. Gallatin Collection.)

André Derain (1880–1954) was an exceptionally strong painter between 1905 and about 1914, and his fauvist works of 1905–1907 are among his most brilliant. His *Henri Matisse* (Fig. 51), an outdoor sketch of his colleague, shows the urgent brushwork and clear fundamental design typical of the early fauvist method. Derain later turned to less turbulent expression, adopting an attractive neoclassical mode which brought him great popularity.

The intensity of fauvist color and brushwork demanded an equally high order of emotional focus, and almost none of the group could retain the alliance. Maurice de Vlaminck (1876–1958), one of the most rebellious and antitraditional of the association, abandoned the vivid colors of 1905 and began working in a successful suavely brushed gray-and-brown manner, as in his *Winter Landscape* (Fig. 52). Vlaminck late in his career denounced modern painting subsequent to that of fauvism.

Figure 52. Maurice de Vlaminck. *Winter Landscape,* 1916-17. 21½ × 25½". (Collection, The Museum of Modern Art, New York. Gift of Mr. and Mrs. Walter Hochschild.)

Othon Friesz and Raoul Dufy also waned in vehemence after about 1908. Dufy became recognized as designer of fabrics for couturiers. Kees Van Dongen changed to a popular variant of his original fauvist method, painting nudes and bathers. Other *fauves*, Marquet, Valtat, and Manguin among them, never fully applied the vividness of technique typical of this group.

Georges Rouault (1871–1958) was unique among fauvists for the moral gravity of his subjects. His colleagues painted landscapes, marine scenes, still lifes, and the figure; but his early fauvist works depicted somberly toned images of venal judges, baleful clowns, sordid-looking prostitutes. Many critics have classified Rouault as an expressionist, connecting his bluntness and introspection with modern German art. He turned more and more to religious themes during the 1920s and 1930s, to some extent brightening his colors and building them into impastos, as in the *Head of Christ* (Fig. 53). Rouault is one of the very few strongly original artists of this century who has painted religious themes. He was also an inventive, powerful printmaker.

Figure 53. Georges Rouault. *Head of Christ,* 1938. 41¼ × 29½". (The Cleveland Museum of Art. Gift of Hanna Fund.)

Georges Braque (1882–1963) contributed strongly to the fauvist movement in 1905–1906 but thereafter turned to cubism, the only member of the circle fully to do so.

Fauvism was short-lived as a definitive style and movement; but its linking of the strongest postimpressionist values—the discoveries of Van Gogh, Gauguin, and Cézanne, especially—with early twentieth-century style, and its emphasis on individual exploration of formal problems, have contributed lastingly to the modern tradition.

EXPRESSIONISM IN GERMANY: *DIE BRÜCKE* (THE BRIDGE) AND IN AUSTRIA

The earlier of two important German expressionist movements, an association called *Die Brücke* (The Bridge), arose in Dresden in 1905, the year of the fauvist exhibit at the Salon d'Automne.

Ernst Ludwig Kirchner (1880–1938), Erich Heckel, Karl Schmidt-Rottluff, and Fritz Bleyl founded *Die Brücke*. Otto Mueller, Max Pechstein, Emil Nolde, Cuno Amiet, Axel Galén, and others joined soon afterward. Kirchner and his friends, like their contemporaries, the *fauves*, desired to create a vigorous art which would challenge the static, academic norm prevalent in their country. Also parallel with fauvism was their great stimulation by the postimpressionists, especially Van Gogh and his vivid color and provocative design. But the Germans were struck by the peculiarly emotional canvases of Edvard Munch and James Ensor, and they also searched their own art history in the effort to establish a kind of ethnic rapport with older mystiques. German medieval woodcuts and the prints of Albrecht Dürer stirred them, as did Grünewald's haunting imagery; and the vitality and bluntness of African and Oceanic arts, encountered by Kirchner in the Dresden Ethnological Museum, likewise met their emotional as well as aesthetic response. Such psychological affinities were in keeping with the group's chosen name; for *The Bridge* implied the spanning of distances between creative artists everywhere, the linking of modern with viable older traditions, and the alliance of conscious and unconscious forces.

Kirchner's *Seated Woman* (*Franzi*) (Fig. 54) is strongly characteristic of Bridge expressionism. It has much in common with French fauvism; but it is more provocative for its implicit tensions of mood than is the French art. The jagged planes of clear color correspond to the intensity of the woman subject. The figure relates harshly to surrounding space.

Figure 54. Ernst Ludwig Kirchner. *Seated Woman (Franzi)*, c. 1907.
31¼ × 35¼". (The Minneapolis Institute of Arts. The John R.
Van Derlip Fund.)

Karl Schmidt-Rottluff (b. 1884) in his handling of color also rivaled
the brilliance of the *fauves;* and his prints in the woodcut medium are
equally potent for their black-and-white starkness. He was inspired
by African sculpture (Fig. 55) as well as German medieval arts. His
The Three Kings (Fig. 56) also shows the expressionists' interest in
religious subjects.

Max Pechstein (1881–1955), Erich Heckel (b. 1883), and Otto
Mueller shared these tendencies, but their art was less stridently colorful. Pechstein, although he traveled to the South Pacific and studied
primitive art, is closer to medieval sources. The oldest of the Bridge
painters, Emil Nolde (1867–1956) had independently developed an
almost brutally forceful style, closer to Ensor in touch but more im-

pacted and frenzied, before he briefly worked with the group. Nolde, like Rouault, belongs to a small minority of modern artists whose religious subjects are convincingly expressed.

Most of the Bridge artists settled in Berlin between 1908 and 1910. Their exhibitions were at first ridiculed by the public, but, like the *fauves*, they won a strong, partisan following.

Other outstanding German painters and printmakers, including Paula Modersohn-Becker, Käthe Kollwitz, and Christian Rohlfs, were somewhat allied to Bridge expressionism but did not belong to the association.

Vienna, a city of contradictory cultural makeup at the turn of the century, produced an expressionism generally similar to that of Germany, but with certain special traits. Gustav Klimt, leader of the once avant-garde Viennese *Sezession*, had influenced many of his students with *art nouveau* or *Jugendstil* aesthetic. One of the most talented of these artists was Egon Schiele (1890–1918), who transcended the ornate curvilinearity of *Jugendstil* and evolved a singularly brilliant

Figure 55. Africa, Fang Tribe, Gabon. *Seated Funerary Figure.* Wood, H. 13⅛". (Collection: Mr. Ernst Anspach, New York.)

Figure 56. Karl Schmidt-Rottluff. *The Three Kings*, 1917. Woodcut, 19 9/16 × 15⅜". (Collection: The Museum of Modern Art, New York [Purchase].)

Figure 57. Egon Schiele. *Portrait of his Wife, Edith,* 1915. Tempera, black chalk and watercolor, 19⅜ × 15¼". (Private Collection. Photograph courtesy Marlborough Fine Art Ltd.)

Figure 58. Oskar Kokoschka, *Portrait of Mme Franzos,* 1909. 45 × 32½". (The Phillips Collection, Washington, D.C.)

draftsmanship (Fig. 57). Both Schiele and his young wife died in the terrible influenza epidemic which followed World War I. His art has only recently been internationally acclaimed.

Oskar Kokoschka (b. 1886), an expressionist playwright as well as painter, was the most controversial of artists in a Vienna which clung to the outmoded gayety of its imperial court but also fostered Freudian psychology and the revolutionary music of Arnold Schönberg. Kokoschka's remarkably analytical portraits of 1909–1912, his strongest period for this medium, were often disquieting in their strange vibrancy; but his likeness of Madame Franzos (Fig. 58) is a quieter example whose delicate sitter seems to be cloaked in a deeply personal reverie.

Kokoschka, who was sponsored by admiring Viennese intellectuals, traveled widely in Europe, painting landscapes of London, Paris, Marseilles, and other great cities of Italy and Germany which, because of their incisive capturing of mood, have been called portraits of those places.

Germany's first modern sculptors, Ernst Barlach (1870–1938) and Wilhelm Lehmbruck (1881–1919) were not associated with expressionist groups, but their respective styles convey something of the intensity and pathos of the movement. Barlach, a playwright like Kokoschka, felt an abiding sympathy for displaced, shunned members of society. A deep humanism haunts the expressive, reduced forms of his *Christ and Thomas* (Fig. 59), a work which is characteristic of Barlach's powerful syntheses of the figure and its movement.

Wilhelm Lehmbruck's art also reveals a deep involvement with the emotional states of his subjects (Lehmbruck, agonized by the human sacrifices of World War I, took his own life in 1919). His early style was influenced by Rodin, Maillol, Minne, and perhaps Medardo Rosso; but his late pieces such as *Praying Woman* (Fig. 60) are notably personal in technique and expressive eloquence.

Figure 59. Ernst Barlach. *Christ and Thomas*, 1926. Bronze, H. 18¾". (Collection: Mr. Ernst Anspach, New York.)

Figure 60. Wilhelm Lehmbruck. *Praying Woman*, 1918. Cast stone. (Wilhelm-Lehmbruck-Museum der Stadt Duisburg. Courtesy of Mr. Guido Lehmbruck.)

Certain other German sculptors, among them Georg Kolbe and Gerhard Marcks, were less clearly indicative of expressionist trends, but their art became distinctive and matured in this period.

The *Brücke* expressionists, again in tandem with their fauvist coevals, disbanded before World War I; but several of them continued to work in a manner closely similar to the 1905–1914 aesthetic, attempting to sustain its vividness.

Several German avant-gardists participated in the international dada movement of 1916–1923 and in the surrealist program which followed it. The last distinctively Germanic contribution to precede the disasters of the national socialist régime of the 1930s and 1940s, however, was the *Neue Sachlichkeit* (new objectivity, or new realism). Max Beckmann (1884–1950), George Grosz (b. 1893) and Otto Dix (b. 1891) led an ideological revolt in line and color against the corrupt political forces which, immediately after the first World War, allowed Germany to fall into shocking economic and moral chaos. It must be noted, however, that the *Neue Sachlichkeit* was not, properly speaking, an art movement, nor can we, except in the art of Dix alone, find a distinctively realistic style. Grosz and Beckmann belong to the expressionist tradition, and their art should be studied in that context.

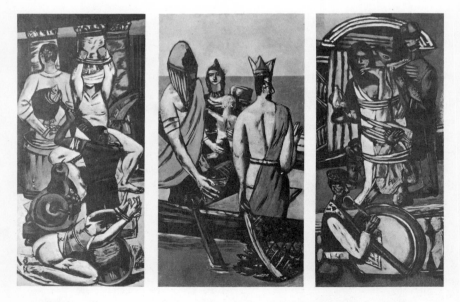

Figure 61. Max Beckmann. *Departure*, 1932-35. Triptych: Center panel 84¾ × 45⅜″. Side panels each 84¾ × 39¼″. (Collection: The Museum of Modern Art, New York.)

Beckmann's contribution was strong and independ
affiliated with the Bridge group, but, despite the
style, his art is more like that of the Bridge than unlike
(Fig. 61), one of a series of dramatic, symbolical tript,
studied for its arcane attributes of iconography but seldom
remarkable stylistic tendencies. Its symbolism, a frightening grotesquery
of sadism which only indirectly involves Beckmann's personal exile from
Germany in the 1930s, belongs to a lengthy Germanic tradition of
eschatology dating from the middle ages. The style unquestionably
owes much to *Brücke* aesthetic, although Beckmann developed independently of that movement and drew upon late impressionism as
transformed by Max Liebermann and other members of the Berlin
Sezession of the 1890s. Expressionism was best known for a time in
the United States in the light of Beckmann's teaching and painting
there following his arrival in 1947.

CUBISM IN FRANCE

Cubism has been one of the two most influential movements in
twentieth century art. Its formulation came between 1907 and 1910
in France, and its principles were extended between 1910 and about
1914. It was again viable after World War I and soon affected almost
every major trend in modern painting and sculpture.

The first stirrings of the great style appeared in the 1906 drawings and paintings of Pablo Picasso (b. 1881), a Spanish artist who
had been academically trained but who was deeply impressed by
postimpressionist and primitive arts after his first visit to Paris in
1900 and his settling there in 1904. His intensely original talents were
emerging in 1906 after the appealing "rose" period paintings, which
were admired by a small group of artists, poets, and collectors. Georges
Braque (1882–1963) had left the fauvist group, and, collaborating
with Picasso in 1907 and later, became co-founder of cubism. The
faceted, turning planes and arcs of this style caused Louis Vauxcelles,
the critic who had labeled the *fauves,* to give the cubists their name
(it is possible that Matisse independently designated it, although he
denied it).

The public and press reacted even more violently against cubism
than it had against fauvism; and, after the renowned exhibit at the
Galerie de la Boétie (the *Section d'Or*) in 1912, an outraged deputy
of the French legislature officially demanded that official sponsorship
should never be extended to this art.

Picasso's early cubism was confirmed and stimulated by African
tribal art (Fig. 62), which shared tendencies already implicit in his

.andling of planes; and he was enchanted by the flatly painted, primitivizing canvases of Henri (*Le Douanier*) Rousseau. Both Picasso and Braque were also instructed by Cézanne's structural innovations; and Braque's landscapes of 1908 reveal this artist's sensitive adaptations of Cézanne's principles.

Figure 62. Africa: Bakota Tribe, Gabon. *Funerary Figure.* Brass and Cooper over Wood, 21½″ H. (Collection: Mr. Ernst Anspach, New York.)

The first great document of the early cubist style is Picasso's *Les Demoiselles d'Avignon* of 1907 (Fig. 63), his largest canvas up until then. Its harsh, aggressive shapes change from left to right within the picture because of the great rapidity of Picasso's development at this stage; but its identity as a cubist work is firm. Picasso was influenced not only by African carvings but by traditional Western figure painting, and perhaps by ancient Iberian sculpture. The jagged planes and arcs of the *Demoiselles* are forcefully reinterpreted in Picasso's bronze

Figure 63. Pablo Picasso. *Les Demoiselles d'Avignon,* 1907. 8′ × 7′ 8″. (Collection, The Museum of Modern Art, New York. Acquired through the Lillie P. Bliss Bequest.)

Woman's Head (Fig. 64) of two years later, the first major sculpture of the cubist movement.

Braque meanwhile paralleled Picasso's tendencies with his landscapes, whose houses and trees were reduced to salient essences of solids, planes, and curves. Their muted colors stood in contrast to their radical innovations in form. Various grays and reserved tones of green, blue, and tan were characteristic.

The second or analytic (sometimes called hermetic) phase of cubism centered in 1910 and 1911. Although cubism was not a fully abstract art in Picasso's and Braque's development of it, such analytic works

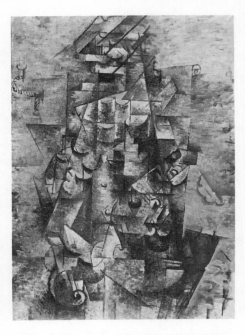

Figure 64. Pablo Picasso. *Woman's Head*, 1909. Bronze, H. 16¼". (Collection: The Museum of Modern Art, New York.)

Figure 65. Georges Braque. *Man with a Guitar*, 1911. 45¾ × 31⅞". (Collection: The Museum of Modern Art, New York. Acquired through the Lillie P. Bliss Bequest.)

as Braque's *Man with a Guitar* (Fig. 65) take natural imagery quite distant from the subject. Multiple or simultaneous views of the figure, rearward planes turned toward the front of the image in facets or prisms, and overlapping shapes demonstrate Braque's intensive analysis of the subject's physical components rather than its appearance.

The cubist style of Picasso and Braque attracted a circle of artists who during 1910–1912 included Juan Gris, Fernand Léger, Marcel Duchamp, Jacques Villon, Robert and Sonia Delaunay, Le Fauconnier, Louis Marcoussis, Auguste Herbin, Roger de La Fresnaye, Jean Metzinger, Albert Gleiszes, André Lhote, and the sculptors Raymond Duchamp-Villon and Archipenko, most of whom exhibited at the controversial *Salle 41* of the Salon des Indépendants in 1911.

A third stage of cubism created the so-called synthetic style of 1912–1914 and its ingenious techniques, *papier collé* and *collage*, in which cutouts of newsprint, shapes of wallpaper or corrugated pasteboard, and other unconventional materials were pasted to the plane of the canvas. Braque appears to be the cubist who discovered this method; but the American self-taught artist Edward Merrill had applied it during the 1880s, using theater posters and birch bark for textures. The Spanish painter, Juan Gris (1887–1927) was especially resourceful in collage, utilizing newsprint legends as in *Breakfast* (Fig. 66). Picasso during this period made reliefs of discarded pieces of wood, paper, and other substances, anticipating constructivist sculpture in Russia and the "combine," or assemblage, reliefs of American artists of the 1950s. He also made a bronze sculpture in the form of an absinthe glass, using a real perforated spoon as one of its elements.

The still-life materials and subjects of synthetic cubism, however, are by no means casual. They refer to objects prominent in the daily

Figure 66. Juan Gris. *Breakfast,* 1914. Pasted paper, crayon and oil on canvas, 31⅞ × 23½". (Collection: The Museum of Modern Art, New York. Acquired through the Lillie P. Bliss Bequest.)

lives of these artists: stringed instruments, playing cards, cigarette packages, and allied items which were attractive as shapes or textures but also intimate in their context.

One of the several substyles of cubism was the so-called "epic" manner of La Fresnaye, Lhote, Metzinger, and others, in which more than characteristic identity of the subject was retained and narratives were used. The opposite trend occurred in *orphism,* or orphist cubism, of Robert and Sonia Delaunay, an early kind of abstract art, as in *Sun Disks* (Fig. 67). Abstraction was not an orthodox purpose of Picasso, Braque, and most other cubists; but certain nonrepresentational movements were to some extent inspired by cubism. Jacques Villon was another member of the group who sometimes worked abstractly.

The American painters Stanton Macdonald-Wright and Morgan Russell, resident in Paris and briefly affiliated with the cubists, developed a method similar to Delaunay's orphism, which they called *syn-*

Figure 67. Robert Delaunay. *Sun Disks*, 1912-13. 53″ diameter. (Collection: The Museum of Modern Art, New York. Mrs. Simon Guggenheim Fund.)

Figure 68. Fernand Léger. *Three Musicians*, 1944. 68½ × 57¼″. (Collection: The Museum of Modern Art, New York. Mrs. Simon Guggenheim Fund.)

chromism. Franz Kupka (1871–1957), a Czech who also knew the cubists, likewise took this style into abstraction. The Russian *rayonnist* Michel Larionov developed a nonobjective style which combined salient aspects of both cubism and Italian futurism.

Fernand Léger (1881–1955) created a vigorous cubism of his own which ranged from abstract canvases in 1913–1914 to machine-inspired interpretations of the human figure beginning in the 1920s. His later *Three Musicians* (Fig. 68) shows the strongly modeled, volumetric manner which is one of the few genuinely machine-influenced aesthetics of this century, although many artists have been stimulated by technological forms.

Marcel Duchamp (b. 1887) is primarily identified with the satirical dada movement of 1916 and later, but he contributed to cubism and was influenced by its analysis of planes in shallow space. His renowned *Nude Descending a Staircase, No. 2* (Fig. 69) is fundamentally a cubist work, although some critics connect it with the contemporary

Figure 69. Marcel Duchamp. *Nude Descending a Staircase, No. 2,* 1912. 58 × 35″. (Philadelphia Museum of Art. The Louise and Walter Arensberg Collection.)

futurist movement in Italy. Actually Duchamp was remarkably independent, and the chief quality of the *Nude Descending* is its
original vigor. Francis Picabia, Duchamp's friend and co-dadaist of
a few years later, also created highly mobile forms, some of them
abstract, at this stage.

Cubism underwent many changes from the time of its early phase
until the advent of World War I, when the several artists disbanded,
some of them going into the armed services. Picasso and Braque after
about 1920, no longer closely collaborating, independently exploited
the style. In the 1920s Picasso worked alternately in a brilliantly colored,
flat manner with sharp-cut images; in a heavily modeled style inspired
by classical sculpture; and in a protosurrealist strain. In the early 1930s
his *Girl Before a Mirror* (Fig. 70) stood out as a singularly potent
example of the late cubist style, its vibrant primary colors reinforced
by an interlacing play of black lines. The rhythms of externalized
glands and the triple image of the face imply a complexly sexual state
of growth.

Braque's late cubist paintings reflect a quieter, steadier tempera-
ment. *The Round Table* (Fig. 71) is an outstanding work of the late
1920s, its interpenetrating but now broad and tilted shapes lucidly

Figure 70. Pablo Picasso. *Girl Before
a Mirror*, 1932. 63¾ × 51¼". (Collection: The Museum of Modern Art,
New York. Gift of Mrs. Simon Guggenheim)

Figure 71. Georges Braque. *The
Round Table*, 1929. 58 × 45". (The
Phillips Collection, Washington, D.C.)

composed in middle depth and handsome in their restrained, appealing tones.

Picasso again amplified his style in the late 1930s to create an unforgettable monument, *Guernica* (Fig. 72), a violent, half-cubist, half-expressionist indictment of all wars and brutalities against man. Occasioned by the unanticipated bombardment by fascist aircraft of

Figure 72. Pablo Picasso. *Guernica*, 1937. Mural, 11' 6" × 25' 8". (On extended loan to the Museum of Modern Art, New York, from the artist, M. Picasso.)

Guernica, a nonstrategic Basque town, this huge portable mural was created for exhibition at the World Fair in Paris in 1937. Picasso actually intensified the deliberate sense of chaos present in *Guernica* by withholding color and using stark blacks and whites and a myriad of gray tones. The savage, oblique symbolism of this work has never been clarified by Picasso himself; but it may involve his unconscious projection of ancient Spanish mythology as well as his personal ciphers of outrage over the inhumanity of war in general.[1]

Few sculptors belonged to the original cubist group, although a generation of them were affected by its discipline. Picasso himself has made many superb third-dimensional works since he created the *Woman's Head* of 1909. Raymond Duchamp-Villon (1876–1918), victim of a sickness contracted during the first World War, was the first cubist whose main energies went ito sculpture. His *Head of a Horse* (Fig. 73) is characteristic. Brother of Marcel Duchamp and Jacques Villon, he was a collaborator with leading cubists during the formative years of the movement.

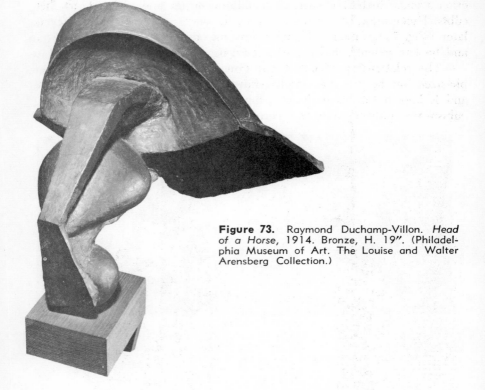

Figure 73. Raymond Duchamp-Villon. *Head of a Horse*, 1914. Bronze, H. 19". (Philadelphia Museum of Art. The Louise and Walter Arensberg Collection.)

Henri Gaudier (Gaudier-Brzeska, 1891–1915), also a victim of World War I, revealed in a few late works the impact of cubism upon his very sensitive talent. Henri Laurens (1885–1954) exhibited with this group after 1912 and throughout his career retained the influence. Ossip Zadkine (b. 1890), Russian by birth, settled in Paris in 1909 and joined the movement. His great influence as a teacher has carried cubism to generations of young artists.

Alexander Archipenko (b. 1887), also Russian-born, briefly associated with the cubists and created a number of works, such as *Silhouette* (Fig. 74), which are early documents of the style. Archipenko, a citizen of the United States since 1928, has been another outstanding teacher.

Jacques Lipchitz (b. 1891) arrived in Paris from Lithuania in 1909, studying at the Ecole des Beaux-Arts but assimilating cubist influences before 1914, when he created bronzes identifiable with the style. Although Lipchitz since the early 1920s has been classified with other trends, including surrealism, expressionism and abstract art, his cubist background sometimes emerges in works of the 1940s and even later (Fig. 75). Lipchitz is one of the major sculptors of this century, and he has saliently influenced American abstract art.

The relationship of Constantin Brancusi to cubism is seldom emphasized, for he was not closely associated with that or any movement and is known for his early contribution to abstract art. Nevertheless, cubism was indispensable as a corollary to his style.

Figure 74. Alexander Archipenko. *Silhouette*, 1910. Chrome-plated bronze. (Hessisches Landesmuseum, Darmstadt, Germany.)

Figure 75. Jacques Lipchitz. *Sacrifice*, 1948. Bronze, 48¾ × 39″. (Albright-Knox Art Gallery, Buffalo, New York.)

Amedeo Modigliani (1884–1920) was a tragically short-lived Italian sculptor-painter who is usually grouped with assorted independent artists in the vague "school of Paris" category. Although he is not to be precisely referred to as a cubist, that definition would connect the one modern source which afforded him strength. His other influences were African primitive art, pre-Hellenic Mediterranean and Italian romanesque carvings, as in his limestone *Head* (Fig. 76). The elegantly mannered *Nude* (Fig. 77), although more ostensibly Italianate than

Figure 76. Amedeo Modigliani. *Head*, 1912
(?). Limestone, H. 25″. (The Solomon R.
Guggenheim Museum Collection, New York.)

the sculpture, shows a subtle adaptation of cubism, imaginatively synthesized.

Marc Chagall, who is discussed later in connection with surrealism, also received instruction
from the cubist method.

The international ascendancy of cubism after
1910 as the most prestigious of modern styles was
reinforced by several critics, poets, private collectors, and dealers who deserve mention. The
writings and encouragement of Guillaume Apollinaire, Max Jacob, André Salmon, Maurice Raynal, Blaise Cendrars, Wilhelm Uhde, and Ger-
trude and Leo Stein were instrumental. Among
early collectors of cubist works were the Steins
and their fellow Baltimoreans, the sisters Cone;
the Russians Morosov and Schoukine; and Wilhelm Uhde. Berthe Weill, Ambroise Vollard, and
Daniel Henry Kahnweiler were among the earlier
dealers in Paris; Herwarth Walden in Berlin, and
the Cassirers; Thannhauser in Munich; and Alfred Stieglitz in New York, who showed avant-
garde European and American works several years before they were
presented in the renowned Armory Show of 1913.

FUTURISM IN ITALY

Italy contributed little to the stream of modern art until after
1900. Aside from Medardo Rosso there were no major artists in late
nineteenth-century Italy.

The most definitive Italian movement of the present century is
futurism, a manifestation which grew not only out of aesthetic drives
but also from the embarrassment of Italy's intellectuals over their
country's lagging technology and worship of its traditional cultural
glories. An antitraditionalist aesthetic, related to nationalist politics,
developed after 1900 and exploded in the first manifesto of futurism
issued by the Milanese poet-critic, Filippo Marinetti.

This bristling document exhorted Italian intellectuals to discard
the outworn legacy of classicism, to oppose the nation's dependency on

Figure 77. Amedeo Modigliani. *Nude*, 1917. 28¾ × 45¼". (The Solomon R. Guggenheim Museum Collection, New York.)

tourism, to exult in physical as well as mental aggressiveness, and to glorify the machine as a new symbol of force. The first manifesto appeared, not in an Italian journal, but in the Parisian review *Le Figaro*, which had published it at the request of Gino Severini, whose career as a painter is chiefly identified with France. The document was soon circulated in Italy, however, and was followed in 1910 by a technical manifesto of futurist painting signed by Umberto Boccioni, Carlo Carrà, Luigi Russolo, and Giacomo Balla. Balilla Pratella's manifesto of futurist music, and its counterpart for sculpture (drafted by Boccioni), appeared in 1912.

Meanwhile, each manifestation of futurism in Italy was met by public outrage which sometimes ended in riots. The attendant publicity, and Marinetti's dramatic appearances in major cities from London to Paris to Moscow, made the Italian movement as internationally renowned, or notorious, as cubism.

It is still by no means certain that futurism got its initial stylistic impetus from cubism; but much evidence supports that art as one of the origins of the Italian trend. Giacomo Balla (1871–1958), oldest of the futurists, had been influenced by *art nouveau* and neoimpressionism.

Figure 78. Giacomo Balla. *Speeding Automobile,* 1912. 21⅞ ×
27⅛". (Collection: The Museum of Modern Art, New York [Pur-
chase].)

Balla's *Speeding Automobile* (Fig. 78) displays several typical
traits. Its theme is a modern, hurtling machine whose velocity is
recorded by vibrating force-lines. The depth, like that of 1912 cubism,
is shallow. Its color, while not brilliant, is brighter than that of the
French style. It is conceived, like cubist painting, largely in terms
of planes. Balla's canvas, in sum, shows much of the spirit of the written
manifestos and their stress upon glorification of the machine, aggressiveness, and speed.

However, the same vector-like force-lines or vibrating silhouettes
and the general urgency of Balla's automobile painting were identically
used in paintings by other futurists, notably Carrà, Severini, and
Russolo, whose customary subjects were not at all the modern machine,
but the traditional human and animal figures. Boccioni (1882–1916),
the most imaginative and disciplined of this group and, with Marinetti,

its co-strategist, contributed one of the greatest of futurist documents with his *Unique Forms of Continuity in Space* (Fig. 79), a running figure; and Boccioni used no less conventional a subject than a bottle to demonstrate growth in space.

It was not the machine which the futurists glorified, but movement. It was the factor of movement, however, which more sharply separated futurism from cubism than did any other quality.

World War I interrupted the growth of this movement as it had expressionism, fauvism, and cubism. Certain of the futurists, true to their principle of aggressiveness, entered the armed services. Boccioni lost his life. Soon after the war, Marinetti became a fascist legislator.

Figure 79. Umberto Boccioni. *Unique Forms of Continuity in Space,* 1913. Bronze, H. 43½". (Collection: The Museum of Modern Art, New York. Acquired through the Lillie P. Bliss Bequest.)

The absence of these two strategists vitiated the futurist trend. Younger adherents during the 1920s and as late as the 1950s undertook to revive futurism; but, even though they presented exhibitions of historical worth, they did little to enrich the living contribution made by the original group.

Futurism enjoyed an influence on Larionov in Russia, a few German expressionists, Wyndham Lewis and the short-lived *vorticist* movement in England, and certain Americans who were studying or working in Europe during the 1910s, Joseph Stella among them. Its exchange of stimulus with cubism in general is problematic, but Duchamp and Picabia, as well as Delaunay, evidently saw in futurism the confirmation of tendencies already present in their painting. Fernand Léger briefly showed possible influences from the Italians, but his concept of the machine as a reference was unlike that of futurism.

EARLY ABSTRACT ART: KANDINSKY AND DER BLAUE REITER

The Bridge artists of Dresden, Germany's first expressionists, had vigorously liberated color, design, and emotional drive in German art. The Munich expressionist group, who called themselves *Der blaue Reiter* (The Blue Rider), made a more momentous contribution to twentieth century tradition. Their leader, Wassily Kandinsky, discovered in 1910 the form which we call abstract, or nonobjective, art. This startling innovation was to become, by midcentury, the leading source of abstract expressionism, of which Kandinsky's 1910–1918 pictures may be considered the preliminary phase.

Most of the Blue Rider artists had known each other before the group was founded in 1911 as successor to the *Neuekünstlervereinigung* (New Artists Association), which, in turn, had grown out of Kandinsky's earlier *Phalanx* circle. Kandinsky, Franz Marc, Paul Klee, August Macke, Gabriele Münter, Alexei von Jawlensky, and Heinrich Campendonk were the principal members. The Blue Rider also attracted American painters, including Marsden Hartley and Lyonel Feininger (who had lived in Germany since early childhood), a few French *fauves* and cubists as well as occasional Bridge expressionists, and the celebrated composer Arnold Schönberg, a serious amateur painter.

Kandinsky by no means created abstract art all at once. He, like Matisse, had first been trained in law and received his early instruction in art at academies (Moscow and Munich, in Kandinsky's case). His early paintings were landscapes and portraits in the acceptable mode of various European academic standards. Kandinsky was briefly influenced, as were most students at the turn of the century, by *art nouveau*. After 1900, he became increasingly inventive in his art, and in 1906, living temporarily in Paris away from Munich, he was stimulated by fauvist color and freedom of touch. Using landscape as his main theme, Kandinsky used increasingly vivid tones and less representational shapes until in 1910 he created a water color which was totally nonobjective. Its remarkably liberated style, which continued until about 1918, is typified by *Light Picture, No. 188* (Fig. 80). It is to be noted that abstract art did not stem from decorative or ornamental forms but from a traditional Western source.

Kandinsky (1866–1944), a Russian-born, keenly intellectual spokesman for modern art, wrote treatises which define the creative artistic process as one which must be based upon inner necessity, upon spiritual

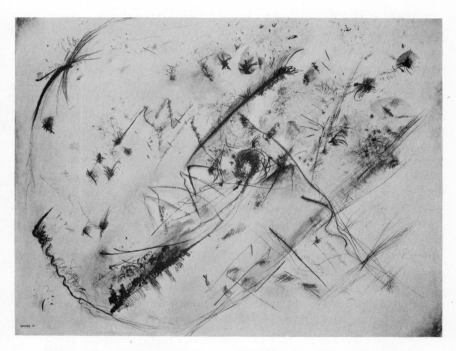

Figure 80. Wassily Kandinsky. *Light Picture, No. 188,* 1913. 30¾ × 39½". (The Solomon R. Guggenheim Museum, New York.)

demands rather than upon the imitation of nature; but he also deeply respected the rhythms of nature itself, which, he observed, had its own particular form.

His abstract style underwent a remarkable transformation before 1920, becoming geometrical in character as in *Circles in a Circle* (Fig. 81). This canvas was painted a year after he joined the faculty of the famous *Bauhaus* at Weimar, a school of design founded by the architect Walter Gropius.

Kandinsky's friend, Franz Marc (1880–1916), similarly arrived at completely nonrepresentational expression, starting with animals in landscapes, which, under Kandinsky's influence and that of cubism and possibly futurism, grew more and more abstract. Marc and his colleague August Macke were killed in the first World War.

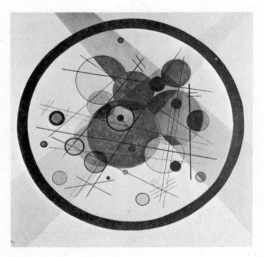

Figure 81. Wassily Kandinsky. *Circles in a Circle*, 1923. 38¾ × 37⅝". (Philadelphia Museum of Art. The Louise and Walter Arensberg Collection.)

Paul Klee (1879–1940), Swiss born but German trained, is often identified with dada and surrealism as well as with abstract art and the Blue Rider. His art is provocatively whimsical in imagery and inventive in technique. Such paintings as *Fish Magic* (Fig. 82) are based upon many sources, including cubism and primitive mask forms as well as the general discipline of German expressionism. Klee's independent, humorously demonic art influenced the surrealists as well as many individual abstract painters.

The Blue Rider membership and affiliates were decidedly international. Lyonel Feininger (1871–1956) was born in America but schooled from childhood in Europe. His entire professional development occurred in Germany. Briefly associated with the original Blue Rider artists in Munich, Feininger was appointed to the Bauhaus faculty in 1919 when the school was founded. He, Kandinsky, Klee, and Jawlensky, who later taught there, were known during the early 1920s as The Blue Four. His prismatic, subtly toned water colors and oils of the 1910s (Fig. 83) disclose both expressionist, orphist-cubist, and possibly futurist influences.

Figure 82. Paul Klee. *Fish Magic*, 1925. 30⅜ × 38½".
(Philadelphia Museum of Art. The Louise and Walter Arensberg Collection.)

Figure 83. Lyonel Feininger. *Side Wheeler*, 1913. 31¾ ×
39⅝". (Courtesy of the Detroit Institute of Arts.)

Marsden Hartley (1887–1943), Albert Bloch, and Konrad Kramer (German born) were other Americans who followed Blue Rider tendencies. Some of Hartley's paintings of 1913–1917 were abstract. Even his late works, such as *Off the Banks at Night* (Fig. 84), show, despite their American subject matter and his commendably independent growth, an affinity for Munich expressionism.

Kandinsky's discovery of abstract form was the greatest Blue Rider legacy to subsequent art; but the group furthered the cause of avant-garde painting and sculpture by exhibiting the works of other new movements along with its own until the War of 1914 disrupted its activities. The writings of Kandinsky and Klee and their teaching at the Bauhaus were also influential on the growth of modern art.

It is generally agreed that Kandinsky was the first to paint non-objectively and to sustain an abstract style. Several other independents, however, arrived almost equally soon at abstraction. Robert Delaunay, Fernand Léger, Jacques Villon, Franz Kupka, Michel Larionov, and the Americans Macdonald-Wright and Morgan Russell, have been

Figure 84. Marsden Hartley. *Off the Banks at Night*, 1942. 30 × 40″. (The Phillips Collection, Washington, D. C.)

mentioned in connection with their cubist-derived abstract art. Most cubists, however, either quickly turned away from nonrepresentational painting once they practiced it, or did not apply it at all.

Other Americans, most of them European trained, may be identified with early abstract art. Few of them consistently followed it, however, after their return to the United States. Arthur G. Dove (1880–1946), who studied with Matisse in Paris before 1910, was a pioneer of nonobjective painting. Patrick Henry Bruce, John Covert, and Arthur B. Carles should also be mentioned. Marsden Hartley, Max Weber, Joseph Stella, Morton Schamberg, Man Ray, and John Marin are more properly to be identified with other avant-garde trends, though each of them to some extent painted abstractions between 1910 and 1920.

SUPREMATISM, CONSTRUCTIVISM, NEOPLASTICISM (DE STIJL)

Definitive contributions to abstract art were made by the movements or styles known as *suprematism, constructivism,* and *neoplasticism (De Stijl)*. The Russian Kasimir Malevich (1878–1935) founded the suprematist style in 1913, using severely geometrical shapes on plain white backgrounds (his canvases were not exhibited until 1915). Such paintings as his *Eight Red Rectangles* (Fig. 85) called for much

Figure 85. Kasimir Malevich. *Eight Red Rectangles,* c. 1914. 22⅜ × 19". (Stedelijk Museum, Amsterdam.)

deliberation and even courage on Malevich's part, for he explained in his book on nonobjectivity that he felt great hesitancy about taking his once-representational manner out of the realm of visual reality and into the unknown world of pure form. *Eight Red Rectangles,* for all its apparent rigidity of shapes, actually contains subtleties which are significant to its effect. The rectangles are slightly trapezoidal, and no two are of exactly the same dimensions. Further, their movement is not, as we might expect, one of conformity to the vertical-horizontal character of the format, but is diagonal. Malevich appears to be the first painter to create an abstraction of purely geometrical elements.

Constructivism was another Russian trend which appeared nearly simultaneously with suprematism. Vladimir Tatlin (1885–1956) founded it, making nonobjective constructions or reliefs of building materials on vertically hung plane surfaces. These reliefs resembled, and may have been in part inspired by, architectural models. El Lissitzky and Alexander Rodchenko were affiliates of constructivism, which was soon led by the brothers Naum Gabo (b. 1890) and Antoine Pevsner (1886–1962). These men issued the movement's first proclamation, which was called the realist manifesto, in 1920. Pure form, the challenge which had led Malevich to his "supreme reality," was sought by Gabo and Pevsner in abstract combinations of modern industrial metals and plastics (Boccioni had earlier advocated the use of antitraditional substances in sculpture).

Russia, which during and immediately after its revolution had encouraged avant-garde expression, developed a reactionary policy in the fine arts in 1921, not finding abstraction useful as an instrument of social propaganda; and Gabo, Pevsner, and other pioneers of this art were constrained to leave the country. After residence elsewhere in Europe, Gabo came to the United States in 1946. His *Linear Construction, Variation* (Fig. 86) illustrates an imaginative, fluid use of contemporary synthetic materials, opened to receive and circulate adjoining space, less severe in concept than the constructivist works of the 1910s. The German Bauhaus at Weimar (later moved to Dessau and to Berlin) became a center of constructivist style during the 1920s, but it was closed by the Nazi government in 1933. The Germans Oskar Schlemmer and Josef Albers (now an American resident), the Hungarian Laszlo Moholy-Nagy, and the Swiss sculptor-painter Max Bill (who is still prominent in European abstraction) were advocates of the constructivist method. These men urged the adaptability of aesthetic to materials and deemphasis of distinctions between fine and industrial arts.

Neoplasticism, better-known by the name of the journal which published its principles, *De Stijl,* evolved in the paintings of Piet Mondrian of Holland (1872–1944) between 1912, when he experienced cubist influence, and about 1917, when his style had become fully geometrical. The movement itself was founded in 1917 with Mondrian, Theo van Doesburg, Bart van der Leck, Georges Vantongerloo, J. P. Oud, and other painters, sculptors, and architects as its members.

Figure 86. Naum Gabo. *Linear Construction, Variation,* c. 1942-43. Plastic and nylon thread construction H. 24½", L. 24¼". (The Phillips Collection, Washington, D. C.)

The severely geometrical *Stijl* aesthetic was based upon the principle of the vertical with an adjoining right-angle horizontal, and the primary colors, blue, red, and yellow (with white and black). Like the suprematists and constructivists, Mondrian and his colleagues searched for a superform independent of the imagery of everyday reality. Mondrian, however, found geometry through a lengthy, intense study of nature, proceeding through a series of landscapes whose forms became increasingly nonobjective, as in the motifs from tree limbs (Fig. 87) and maritime views in which the severe horizon line and horizontal movement of the waves opposed the verticals of the piers of a dock. Mondrian's *Composition* (Fig. 88) shows the full development of neoplasticism, or *De Stijl*, in arrangements of rectangles and rectilinear strips.

Victor Servranckx (b. 1897), an independent Belgian artist, developed a similarly geometrical style in the early 1920s, combining rectangular and circular motifs; and Alberto Magnelli (b. 1888), an Italian who has worked chiefly in Paris, also practiced a less severe nonobjective art during the late 1910s.

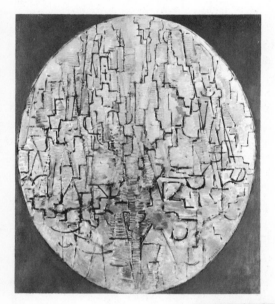

Figure 87. Piet Mondrian. *Oval Composition (Trees)*, 1913. 37 × 30¾". (Stedelijk Museum, Amsterdam.)

Figure 88. Piet Mondrian. *Composition*, 1929. 17¾ × 17¾". (The Solomon R. Guggenheim Museum, New York. Gift, Katherine S. Dreier Estate.)

EARLY ABSTRACT SCULPTURE

Sculpture also has a significant history in early abstract art. Tatlin, Archipenko, Brancusi were among the earliest practitioners, although the priority is imperfectly known. Louis Chauvin (b. 1889) should also be mentioned.

Constantin Brancusi (1876–1957) is outstanding among the first nonobjective sculptors, though many of his characteristic pieces derive from natural objects. A Romanian who settled in Paris in 1904, he studied with an academician but was strongly conditioned by Rodin's ideas. It is probable that Brancusi was affected, as were so many young artists of the time, by the art of both Aristide Maillol (1861–1944) and Emile–Antoine Bourdelle (1861–1929). The differences between the styles of these two men are often overemphasized, and both Bourdelle's furtherance of Rodin's principles of mobility and broken surface, and Maillol's supposed rejection of those traits and his alleged serenity, are sometimes inexactly understood. As it applies to Brancusi's possible response, the main conflict is a more distantly conceptual one. The forms of Maillol's *Pomona* (Fig. 89) are by no means unsensuous, but they are more nearly self-contained as forms than are their counterparts in Bourdelle's *Herakles* (Fig. 90); and they invite little speculation about extra-artistic values, whereas the formal impact of the *Herakles* leads to additional, nonformal inquiry.

Brancusi's aesthetic, which is thought to have been based partly upon his concern for the essences of organic forms, is little closer to one of the above positions than to the other. His works of the 1910s and later pieces, such as *Bird in Space* (Fig. 91), are innovating in their crystallization of growth and movement as the effects of interior attributes rather than as the reduced images of visible action.

Brancusi's abstractions reached popularity among collectors in the United States before they were well-known in France. The *Bird in Space* accidentally won Brancusi a popular following in America when, after the customs authorities denied its eligibility for passing duty free as a work of art, a widely publicized lawsuit resulted, ending in recognition of the *Bird* as a sculpture instead of taxable industrial metal.

The influence of African, Oceanic, and other primitive arts upon *fauves*, expressionists and cubists has been referred to. Brancusi and other abstract sculptors were also inspired by pre-Hellenic carvings like *A Man Playing a Syrinx* (Fig. 92) from the Cycladic Islands of Greece. Jean (Hans) Arp (1887–1966), whose earliest, free-form reliefs in wood are associated with the dada movement of 1916, was impressed by the radical purity of such non-classical art, as shown in his *Torse-Gerbe* (Fig. 93).

Figure 89. Aristide Maillol. *Pomona aux bras tombante*, 1910. Bronze, H. 66". (Collection of Mr. David Lloyd Kreeger, Washington, D. C.)

Figure 90. E. Antoine Bourdelle. *Herakles, Archer,* 1909. Bronze, H. 14¾". (Courtesy of The Art Institute of Chicago. A. A. Munger Collection.)

Figure 91. Constantin Brancusi. *Bird in Space,* 1925. Polished bronze, marble base, H. 49¾". (Philadelphia Museum of Art. The Louise and Walter Arensberg Collection.)

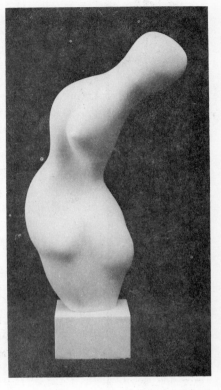

Figure 92. Cycladic Figurine. *A Man Playing a Syrinx*, c. 2500 B.C. (Collection: the Detroit Institute of Arts. Photograph André Emmerich Gallery, New York.)

Figure 93. Jean Arp. *Torse-Gerbe*, 1958. Marble, H. 44½". (Courtesy Sidney Janis Gallery, New York.)

DADA AND SURREALISM

Dada was a revolutionary movement in literature and art founded in Zurich in 1916 by the Romanian poet Tristan Tzara and his compatriot, Marcel Janco; the German writers Richard Huelsenbeck and Hugo Ball; the Alsatian Jean (Hans) Arp, whose sculpture has been mentioned; and Sophie Taeuber, who married Arp. The name dada, meaning an infantile sound or a hobby-horse, allegedly was taken at random from a French-language dictionary, a gesture which characterizes much of the playfulness and irony of the movement. These brilliant independents centered at the Cabaret Voltaire in Zurich, where they worked as waiters and entertainers and where they propounded their antimilitaristic, antiaesthetic aesthetic. In spite of the ostensibly negative attitude thus implied, the dadaists provided the modern tradition a refreshing, satirical program. Kindred movements appeared elsewhere in Europe and in New York until 1923, after which dada's increased membership helped to found the surrealist movement in Paris.

Marcel Duchamp, Picabia, Man Ray, Morton Schamberg, and Walter Arensberg in New York, and Max Ernst and Johannes Baargeld in Cologne, as well as Kurt Schwitters in Hanover, conducted dada manifestations. André Breton, Louis Aragon, and Philippe Soupault led a Paris contingent.

The visual arts of dada were characterized by Duchamp's "ready-mades," deliberately absurd assemblages of utensils or bicycle parts, sometimes elegantly mounted on sculpture stands or placed in glass cages; Schwitter's *Merzbilder,* "junk pictures," or collages of trash, and Ernst's similarly satirical works; and clothing dummies and large reproductions of old masters with sculptural or painted adducements.

There were also behavioral arts. The dadaists held mock fist fights in public and cheered or jeered at illogical junctures in movies, and otherwise engaged in planned disruptions of the public peace. A brilliant, pun-laden antilogic accompanied much of their creative effort.

The nihilistic or otherwise negative aspects of dada have been stressed out of proportion to the invigorating effects which this movement and its personalities have exerted on later arts. The presence of Marcel Duchamp in New York during many of the years since about 1915 has in itself had far-reaching influences on recent avant-garde trends.

Surrealism, one of the most energetically publicized and least well understood movements of recent times, was proclaimed in Paris in 1924 by its literary head, André Breton. Its official journal was *La Révolution.* The first major surrealist exhibition appeared in 1925 and included the works of Arp, Ernst, Klee, De Chirico, Man Ray, André Masson, Joan Miró, Pierre Roy, and Picasso (not all of whom were members of the association). Later affiliates included Yves Tanguy, René Magritte, Salvador Dali, Paul Delvaux, and Matta.

It should be understood that surrealism was fundamentally a literary and romantic movement, and from the outset, certain of its advocates, beginning with André Breton, tended to confuse the respective values of literature, art, and Freudian psychology, the latter being a much-publicized but not especially well-understood attribute of the program. The glibly naturalistic techniques of certain members were on principle inadequate vehicles for the programmatic transcription of bizarre dream imagery or conscious probing of the unconscious.

Much of the valid painting was done by independent artists like Picasso and the Italian Giorgio de Chirico (b. 1888), who were antecedents of surrealism but not members of the movement. De Chirico's singularly melancholy landscapes of 1909–1915 (Fig. 94) provided

Figure 94. Giorgio de Chirico. *The Anguish of Departure,* 1913-14. 33½ × 27¼". (Albright-Knox Art Gallery, Buffalo, New York. The Room of Contemporary Art Fund.)

an authentic source for several orthodox surrealists whose talents failed to match its mystique.

Similarly, the Russian-born Marc Chagall (b. 1889), who was claimed by this movement but not fully identifiable with it, has contributed to modern art a unique fantasy and a commensurately imaginative technique, as in his *Half-Past Three: The Poet* (Fig. 95). Chagall's modernity, especially his cubist-inspired sense of structure, might have been paid more heed by those who indulged in heavy-handed mystification.

Among the regular members, Joan Miró (b. 1893), a keenly original Spanish artist, has contributed not only to surrealism but to the broader tradition of modern abstract art, as in his *Personage in the Presence of Nature* (Fig. 96). Max Ernst has sometimes lapsed into the labored modeling and forced specifics of realism typical of the least creative aspects of this movement; but he has more often, as in his *Birds above*

Figure 95. Marc Chagall. *Half-Past Three: The Poet,* 1911. 77½ × 57½". (Philadelphia Museum of Art. The Louise and Walter Arensberg Collection.)

Figure 96. Joan Miró. *Personage in the Presence of Nature,* 1935. 29¾ × 41½". (Philadelphia Museum of Art. The Louise and Walter Arensberg Collection.)

the Forest (Fig. 97), retained the whimsy of his dada phase. Ernst has also contributed significantly to contemporary sculpture.

Figure 97. Max Ernst. *Birds above the Forest,* 1929. 31¾ × 25¼". (Collection: The Museum of Modern Art, New York. Katherine S. Dreier Bequest.)

Alberto Giacometti (1901–1966), a deeply gifted Swiss sculptor, transcended the literary, pseudo-Freudian obscurities of surrealism to independently create some of the most serious figural pieces of the mid-twentieth-century (Fig. 98). His melancholy is unforced and singularly expressive. Another distinguished contributor to the style of this movement was the Frenchwoman Germaine Richier (1904-1959), whose eerie, unstable images are hauntingly impressive.

Unfortunately, many persons have come to know surrealism through the public antics of Salvador Dali (b. 1904), a latecomer to surrealism whose overworked painting mode has contributed little to the distinction of the movement (Fig. 99). A much more convincing superrealism is that of Pierre Roy (1880–1950), who anticipated the realist method which few orthodox surrealists were actually able to make viable.

Matta (Matta Echuarren, b. 1912) is one of the few younger painters whose main development may be associated with surrealism. His tendencies, however, are altogether abstract, and he has significantly contributed to that tradition.

Figure 98. Alberto Giacometti. *Large Head,* 1960. Bronze, H. 37". (The Phillips Collection, Washington, D. C.)

Figure 99. Salvador Dali. *Paranoiac Image,* 1934. 6¼ × 8 11/16". (Courtesy Wadsworth Atheneum, Hartford.)

The influences of surrealism have been diverse. Fortunately, its higher characteristics rather than its less convincing orthodoxy of extra-artistic values have affected certain recent artists, especially the New York action painters and sculptors; and these men have matched the unique challenge of subconscious image seeking by providing an adequate technique.

OTHER TRENDS FROM THE 1920s TO THE 1940s

Almost every significant trend of the 1905–1914 phase of modern art was amplified between the early 1920s and the years of World War II. The growth of expressionism, cubism, early abstract art, dada, and surrealism in Europe has already been considered. Many American artists, too, had experienced this development while working or studying abroad. Others observed the exhibitions at the *291* gallery of Alfred Stieglitz in New York, who several years before the celebrated Armory Show of 1913 had shown works by Picasso, Matisse, and other European vanguardists as well as promising Americans. The Armory Show, an exhibition of unprecedentedly great scope, had brought before the American public works representative of nearly every contemporary style (by no means all of which were revolutionary). Some 1,250 paintings and sculptures were shown in New York, and a reduced collection was sent to Chicago and Boston, being seen by about 300,000 persons. Much of the response was hostile and given astonishingly full coverage in the press; but certain critics were won over, a few adventuresome new collectors appeared, and hundreds of American artists were instructed. The Association of American Painters and Sculptors, which had organized the Armory Show partly out of protest against the restrictive exhibition policies of academic forces, had triumphed.

The nineteenth-century tradition of American adaptation and re-interpretation of European tendencies continued into the 1920s and 1930s. John Marin (1870–1953) based his primarily expressionistic style on several trends he had studied during his visits to Europe soon after 1900. An extraordinarily vigorous practitioner of water color, Marin, in paintings like *Ship, Sea and Sky Forms* (Fig. 100), enriched an art which led to his international recognition.

The international character of expressionism during the 1920s and 1930s affected the development of Max Weber and Marsden Hartley, both of whom had received early impetus from this style around 1910.

Arthur Dove, Arthur B. Carles, Samuel Halpert, Oscar Bluemner, Abraham Walkowitz, and Joseph Stella were among the scores of American artists whose growth during this period was impelled by

Figure 100. John Marin. *Ship, Sea and Sky Forms,* 1923. Water color, 13½ × 17". (The Columbus Gallery of Fine Arts, Columbus, Ohio. Ferdinand Howald Collection.)

one or another avant-garde European tradition which they had known before 1920.

Realism, a late-nineteenth-century trend much favored in the United States, was most cogently exploited during the 1920s and early 1930s, not in the Eakins-Homer tradition, but in the curiously abstract adaptation of it by the *immaculates* or *precisionists,* a group of independents including Charles Demuth (1883–1935), Charles Sheeler (b. 1883), Georgia O'Keeffe (b. 1887), Preston Dickinson (1891–1930), and Niles Spencer (d. 1952). The immaculates' method typically imposed upon landscape or architectural forms, and sometimes still lifes and figures, a sharp-cut lighting, clarity of silhouette, and rhythmic composition which revealed the artists' conversance with abstraction. The German *Neue Sachlichkeit* of the early 1920s has occasionally been compared with this American movement, but the analogy is neither stylistically nor emotionally valid.

Two less formalizing realists of this period were Charles Burchfield (b. 1893) and Edward Hopper (1882-1967). Both worked in an essentially romantic variant of their tradition, but neither was close to the nineteenth century. Burchfield's distinctively mysterious water colors, such as *Night of the Equinox* (Fig. 101), disclose an underlying *art nouveau* influence coupled with his own sensitive feeling for pattern as well as mood.

Hopper's style, which conveys a bleakness of a different order than Burchfield's, deals with the exteriorized realities of his subjects

Figure 101. Charles Burchfield. *Night of the Equinox*, 1917-1955. Water color, 40 × 52″. (Collection of the Sara Roby Foundation, New York.)

(Fig. 102) but shows a selective restraint in its artist's attempt to depict those forms.

Ben Shahn's paintings during the early 1930s displayed a deliberately primitivizing realism coupled with social allegory. His renowned Saccho and Vanzetti trial pictures (Fig. 103) are decidedly sophisticated, however, in their almost abstract discipline of spacing and clear-cut distribution of dark and light contrasts. Shahn (b. 1898) has been classified as a "social realist"; but his style, which has become in-

Figure 102. Edward Hopper. *Sunday*, 1926. 29 × 34″. (The Phillips Collection, Washington, D. C.)

creasingly abstract since the 1930s, is too clearly ordered to be grouped with a majority of the indiscriminately detailed and illustrational manners used by hundreds of so-called social realists who painted during this phase of American art.

The New Deal of President Franklin Roosevelt in the 1930s was the first administration of the United States to recognize and massively support the American artist. A widespread program of mural and easel painting and sculpture was sponsored by the Federal Art Project for public buildings. This undertaking encouraged hundreds of artists. While the terms *social realism* and *American Scene* are often categorically extended to all of this art, the several styles used in it were variegated and not nearly so distinctive as the subject matter. Several painters who worked in the Project were to participate later in the abstract expressionist movement of the 1940s.

The Mexican government also sponsored an abundant mural-painting program during the 1930s which has remained active. Its

Figure 103. Ben Shahn. *The Passion of Saccho and Vanzetti*, 1931-32. Tempera on canvas, 84½ × 48″. (From the Sacco-Vanzetti series of 23 paintings. Collection of the Whitney Museum of American Art, New York. Gift of Edith and Milton Lowenthal in memory of Juliana Force.)

thematic character has generally been propagandistic. Among its outstanding artists are the late Diego Rivera, David Siquieros, José Clemente Orozco, and Rufino Tamayo. Tamayo is known in the United States and Europe for easel paintings of a distinctly modern style.

Avant-garde trends in sculpture enjoyed little practice in the United States during this period. In Europe, Matisse, the only serious practitioner of sculpture among the former *fauve* group, continued until about 1935 to make small bronze figures. The Bauhaus constructivists were displaced by the Nazi abolition of the school in 1933. Meanwhile, Arp, Giacometti, Lipchitz, Brancusi, and others enriched their styles independently. The Spaniard Julio Gonzalez (1876–1942), who had been developing ironworking techniques since the 1910s, made significant contributions to its methodology around 1930. Picasso, working with his compatriot, promptly created some especially striking, openwork rod sculptures in forged and joined techniques.

Henry Moore (b. 1898), one of the outstanding sculptors of the twentieth century, gave his first one-man show in 1927 and was internationally recognized before the advent of World War II. He allied several impressive influences, including cubism, surrealism, African and Precolumbian carvings, and English medieval sculpture, synthesizing these into an independent, massive expression notable for its fluidity of silhouette and perforations which unite volumes with space (Archipenko had made use of void shapes in the 1910s). Moore's *Recumbent Figure* (Fig. 104) is characteristic of the form which he also used in fully abstract works as early as the 1920s.

Figure 104. Henry Moore. *Recumbent Figure,* 1938. Green Hornton stone, L. c. 54". (Reproduced by courtesy of the Trustees of the Tate Gallery, London.)

The Englishwoman Barbara Hepworth (b. 1903) is another distinguished sculptor whose development and early recognition came during this period.

Few American sculptors ventured into avant-garde expression during the 1920s. Archipenko settled in New York in 1923, strengthening the tradition by his presence; but his students were some time in producing. William Zorach (1887–1966) turned from painting to direct carving in stone about 1924, evolving a glyptic, simplified realism. Heinz Warneke worked in a similar vein. John Flannagan (1895-1942) very economically articulated animal images from boulders or blocks, retaining the basic shape of his material. His *Monkey and Young* (Fig. 105) is characteristic of a style which later influenced several abstract sculptors.

The Frenchman Gaston Lachaise (1882–1936) and Elie Nadelman, a Pole, each brought to the United States a blend of *art nouveau* and cubism. Lachaise, the more vigorous of the two men, created extraordinarily rhythmic, full-volumed bronzes of women (Fig. 106). Nadelman's art was more compact, almost hermetically streamlined.

American nonobjective sculpture was notably scarce until Alexander Calder (b. 1898) created his first mobiles in 1931. These flat, clear-cut metallic shapes, boldly spanning lengths of touch- and wind-sensitive rods, were unique in sculptural history and have enhanced the prestige

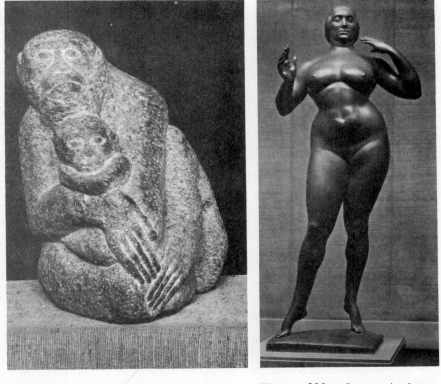

Figure 105. John B. Flannagan. *Monkey and Young,* 1932. Granite, H. 15". (Addison Gallery of American Art, Phillips Academy, Andover, Massachusetts.)

Figure 106. Gaston Lachaise. *Standing Woman,* 1912-27. Bronze, H. 70". (Collection of the Whitney Museum of American Art, New York.)

of American art among Europeans. Calder's aesthetic influences were cubism, Miró, and constructivism; but the concept of an alive, unmechanized, sculptural form is singularly original. This engineer-trained artist also developed stabile sculptures whose shapes resemble those of the mobiles but are more compactly grouped. *Red Flock* (Fig. 107) is an excellent example of his art.

Stuart Davis (1894–1964) was one of the most consistent of American avant-garde painters of the interval between the two world wars, and his presence in New York was cogent to the rise of abstract art in the 1940s. Davis's influences were fauvism, early and late or flat cubism, and probably *De Stijl;* but his pristine shapes and bright, lively colors, typically suggesting a theme with visually real context, belong to a relatively precise or geometrical abstraction which has still enjoyed less viability in the United States than have more liberated nonobjective modes. The distinctive manner of Davis is shown in his *Owh! in San Pao* (Fig. 108). This strain of sharply defined, geometrically formalized

Figure 107. Alexander Calder. *Red Flock,* c. 1949-50. Metal and wire mobile, H. 33½″. (The Phillips Collection, Washington, D. C.)

Figure 108. Stuart Davis.
Owh! in San Pao, 1951. 52½
× 41¾". (Collection of the
Whitney Museum of American
Art, New York.)

abstraction was also sponsored by G. L. K. Morris and Albert Gallatin, who, with others, in 1937 founded the American Abstract Artists group. The arrival meanwhile of several recently displaced Europeans, including Piet Mondrian and the constructivist Josef Albers, gave the formalized abstract method support.

The most viable movement in the history of American art, however, which stemmed from the liberating aesthetic of Kandinsky rather than from the severer styles, was being formulated just as the United States entered World War II: abstract expressionism.

FOOTNOTE

[1]See the psychological studies by Juan Larrea, *Guernica* (New York: Curt Valentin, 1947) and Rudolf Arnheim, *Picasso's Guernica: The Genesis of a Painting* (Berkeley: University of California Press, 1962).

6

Abstract Expressionism and Later Arts

The most dynamic movement of the 1940s and subsequent years has been abstract expressionism, a development which matured in New York between about 1942 and 1948 and soon affected the styles of painters everywhere. Europeans for the first time looked upon the United States as the leading source of world art. Other challenging trends have since appeared; but abstract expressionism has probably not yet made its ultimate historical impact.

The modern sources of this explosive art are Kandinsky's paintings of the 1910s; Marcel Duchamp's dadaism and the surrealism of Miró and Klee; and the teaching of Hans Hofmann. Each major exponent of the style, however, felt a unique combination of these and certain additional stimuli. These artists called upon every imaginative reference at their disposal, probing unconscious imagery in their anxiety to create forms which had never been exteriorized.

The founders and early practitioners of abstract expressionism were Arshile Gorky, Hans Hofmann, Jackson Pollock, Robert Motherwell, Willem DeKooning, Philip Guston, Bradley Walker Tomlin, Adolf Gottlieb, William Baziotes, Mark Rothko, James Brooks, Barnett Newman, Ad Reinhardt, Theodoros Stamos, Franz Kline, Sam Francis, Clyfford Still, and Paul Burlin (other names might well be added). These men are sometimes called action painters, a term first used by the critic Harold Rosenberg. Most of them had earlier painted representational pictures, but each found his own way to the generally nonobjective aesthetic of this new style.

Arshile Gorky (1940–1948), a pioneer of the movement, was close to Kandinsky's and the surrealists' method of automatic expression of unconscious imagery. His *The Betrothal, II* (Fig. 109) discloses a deeply personal emotional state which is spontaneously projected in elegant, linear configurations and muted tones of yellow, tan, violet, and green.

Figure 109. Arshile Gorky. *The Betrothal, II,* 1947. 50¾ × 38″. (Collection of the Whitney Museum of American Art, New York.)

These are ciphers of the painter's mind, eye, and hand, not descriptively interpreted forms. This intense, urgently painted work is not intended to correspond to the literature of Freudian psychology, although it is related to it.

One of the giants of abstract expressionism or action painting was Jackson Pollock (1912–1956), who created his *Cathedral* (Fig. 110) in the controversial technique of dripping and splashing filaments and spots of color on the horizontally placed canvas instead of directly using the brush. This radical procedure was no more or less suitable to Pollock's turbulent drives, however, than was Seurat's deliberate spotting of pigments essential to neoimpressionist purposes. A distinctive order, too, is present in the intricate, space-dissolving mesh of *Cathedral's* surface; not the order of traditional painting nor even of some recent art, but an order of an innovating and powerful kind.

The art of Robert Motherwell (b. 1915) is more measured and ideographic than Pollock's, its tempo less urgent. Yet his *Elegy to the Spanish Republic XXXIV* (Fig. 111) reveals an equally great tension more subtly carried out. Small, unaggressive forms are being slowly crushed between jagged vertical bands. The colors themselves, somber blacks and dense warm earth tones, imply a mute violence.

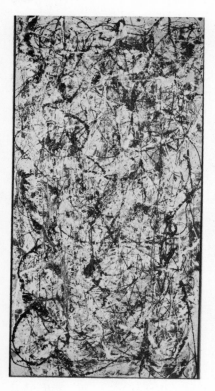

Figure 110. Jackson Pollock. *Cathedral*, 1947. Oil and mixed media on canvas, 71 × 35″. (Dallas Museum of Fine Arts. Gift of Mr. and Mrs. Bernard J. Reis.)

Motherwell, a distinguished writer and speaker as well as painter, has been instrumental in the widespread acceptance of the movement.

Willem DeKooning (b. 1904) was born and trained in Holland. Like most abstract expressionists, DeKooning at first painted representational works, and his early drawings of the figure are almost neoclassical in their elegance. Exactly the opposite is the tortured, propelled image of his *Woman and Bicycle* (Fig. 112). Most of his works are fully abstract, but he and other action painters have also made, not the visual likeness of persons and objects, but their emotional responses to that visual reality. DeKooning's style is relentlessly savage, combining surrealist and expressionist values.

Hans Hofmann (1880–1966) conducted his own art school in pre-National Socialist Germany but withdrew to the United States in the early 1930s and became an invigorating teacher of abstract painting in New York and elsewhere. His style is closer to its fauvist and Blue Rider origins, especially in its vivid color, than is much American abstract expressionism. His *Exuberance* (Fig. 113) displays a liberated

Figure 111. Robert Motherwell. *Elegy to the Spanish Republic XXXIV*, 1953-54. 80 × 100″. (Albright-Knox Art Gallery, Buffalo, New York. Gift of Seymour H. Knox.)

adaptation of cubist structure. Hofmann's aesthetic directly influenced the earliest phase of action style.

The impact of Franz Kline's bristling black-and-white canvases such as *New York* (Fig. 114) is instantly challenging. His is one of the bluntest, least meditative approaches of his group and one which makes clear the meaning of "action" as a name for the style. The thrusting motion of the brush in its velocity leaves a record of the painter's physical motion. Kline (1910–1962) suggests, but does not imitate, the girders and towers of the city in which he lived.

Bradley Walker Tomlin (1889–1953) also developed an independent style within the broad reference of abstract expressionism. His staccato, ribbon-like maze of white strokes forms a structure whose dark intervals are comparatively austere, revealing, even if indirectly, this artist's former interest in cubist and *Stijl* methods, as in *Number 1* (Fig. 115).

Figure 112. William DeKooning. *Woman and Bicycle*, 1952-53. 76½ × 49". (Collection of the Whitney Museum of American Art, New York.)

Figure 113. Hans Hofmann. *Exuberance*, 1955. 50 × 40". (Albright-Knox Art Gallery, Buffalo, New York. Gift of Seymour H. Knox.)

Figure 114. Franz Kline. *New York*, 1953. 79 × 50½″. (Albright-Knox Art Gallery, Buffalo, New York. Gift of Seymour H. Knox.)

Figure 115. Bradley Walker Tomlin. *No. 1*, 1951. 78 × 42″. (Munson-Williams-Proctor Institute, Utica, New York. Edward W. Root Bequest.)

Certain abstract expressionists were stimulated by the emotive as well as the formal qualities of primitive arts, Adolf Gottlieb being one of them. The totemic power of that source appealed to Mark Rothko (b. 1903). Like Mondrian and Malevich, this painter has intensely probed for an independent, unknown form. In his art he expunges nonessentials and establishes, as in *Green and Maroon* (Fig. 116), an externalized emotional state which is compactly reduced to looming, paired rectangles. These are enriched by Rothko's delicate blurring of initially sharp edges and by his vibrant, subtly broken color.

Mark Tobey (b. 1890), a West Coast painter who won the grand international prize at the Venice Bienale in 1958 (Whistler had been the last American to do so), does not identify himself with abstract expressionism; but European artists do, and his own pioneering in "white writing" abstraction is relevant to the growth of the tradition in the United States. Tobey's *Universal Field* (Fig. 117) is characteristic

Figure 116. Mark Rothko. *Green and Maroon*, 1953. 90¾ × 54½". (The Phillips Collection, Washington, D. C.)

Figure 117. Mark Tobey. *Universal Field*, 1949. 28 × 44". Tempera and pastel on cardboard. (Collection of the Whitney Museum of American Art, New York.)

of his painting, which developed during the 1930s independently of New York sources.

A substyle of abstract expressionism has been called abstract impressionism. This manner, usually less vehemently projected than the parent style, suggests the presence of an image which is blurred or otherwise obscured. Larry Rivers and John Ferren developed this tendency.

Scores of additional artists contributed to the astonishing viability of abstract expressionism and its variants. Most of the early practitioners of this style who are mentioned above were recognized throughout the world in the 1950s and were honored by the highest international awards.

RECENT AMERICAN SCULPTURE

Contemporary sculpture enjoyed a similar efflorescence. The provocative works of David Smith, Theodore Roszak, Seymour Lipton, Herbert Ferber, Isamu Noguchi, David Hare, Ibram Lassaw, Reuben Nakian, and many other American artists approximated the power displayed by action painting. Their art, too, has been influential overseas.

The recent and older sources of the new sculpture were more diverse than those of the painting. The general influences included, interestingly enough, the art of certain painters, especially Kandinsky, Picasso, and Mondrian, among others; and the ironworking methods of Julio Gonzales (already mentioned) and the intensely fertile art of Jacques Lipchitz, who had for some years worked in the United States. Giacometti, Brancusi, Arp, Duchamp, Archipenko, Gabo, Henry Moore, Alexander Calder, and Flannagan stimulated several of them; and medieval and primitive arts afforded another reference.

Welding and other metalworking methods appealed to a majority of the abstract sculptors of the 1950s, but some worked in more traditional techniques.

David Smith (1906–1965) was exceptionally forceful. His *Voltron XVIII* (Fig. 118), for example, is unforgettably harsh and tension-filled. Smith's persistent concerns over past brutalities and contemporary threats to man were a strong, nonvisual impetus to the jagged strength of his style. His art has strongly influenced many European sculptors.

Theodore Roszak (b. 1907), Seymour Lipton (b. 1903), and David Hare (b. 1917) use similarly harsh forms but with independent emotional and technical shadings. Herbert Ferber (b. 1906) works in open, twisted calligraphic shapes which imply a personal symbolism. Ibram Lassaw (b. 1913) and Richard Lippold (b. 1915) are closer

Figure 118. David Smith. *Voltron XVIII,* 1963. Steel, H. 110⅞". (Marlborough-Gerson Gallery Inc., New York.)

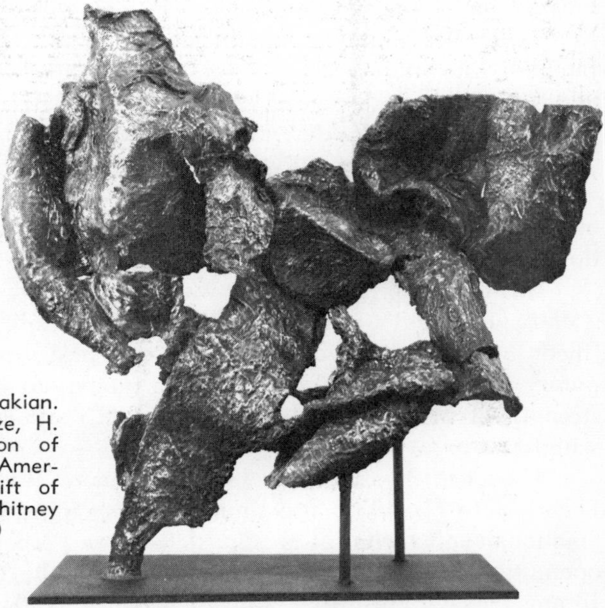

Figure 119. Reuben Nakian. *Olympia,* 1960-62. Bronze, H. 72", W. 72". (Collection of the Whitney Museum of American Art, New York. Gift of the Friends of the Whitney Museum [and purchase].)

to a formalized structural aesthetic, evidently one combining cubist and constructivist principles. They fashion cagelike or openwork assemblages of rods and wires which are sometimes finished with precious metals.

Reuben Nakian (b. 1897), who studied with Lachaise and was influenced by John Flannagan, developed the singular, baroque-expressionist manner shown in his *Olympia* (Fig. 119). Like most of his contemporaries, Nakian favors roughly textured surfaces, although he typically works in bronze rather than the more popular welded metals.

The trends of recent American sculpture, which indicate a liberated concept of the roles of space, materials, and personal expressiveness, have parallels in action painting.

RECENT EUROPEAN ART

The full impact of abstract expressionism reached most parts of the world during the 1950s. Its powerful, commanding presence seemed to meet emotional as well as professional needs. In certain places the American styles were directly influential or confirmed indigenous tendencies not yet exploited. More formalized trends, especially those evolved from *Stijl* or constructivist approaches, were accelerated by the impetus of the other activity. But everywhere the nonobjective tradition was prevalent; and even in the few ineffectual attempts to "bring back the figure," as certain forces of reaction nostalgically put it, the discipline of abstraction was to some degree applied.

England, where most artists before the mid-1930s had not warmly responded to avant-garde continental painting and sculpture, has produced a postwar art of vigor and imaginativeness. The spiky and threatening grotesquery of Graham Sutherland (b. 1903) and the sardonic figural images of Francis Bacon (b. 1910 in Ireland) extend from the British tradition of fantasy and demonic art epitomized by Blake, Fuseli, and Samuel Parker, but both men have undergone the effects of recent structural disciplines. Ben Nicholson (b. 1894), widely recognized before the war for his distinctive, cubist-inspired canvases and reliefs, and Stanley William Hayter, a singularly inventive printmaker who has long resided in Paris, have been influential upon a generation of younger English artists. John Piper, William Coldstream, C. R. W. Nevinson, and John Tunnard were also well-known during the 1930s. Avant-garde trends in British painting include, as they do elsewhere, both formalized and liberating styles and substyles of nonfigural or semiabstract art. Among the many distinguished practitioners are Victor Pasmore, Alan Davie, Adrian Heath, William Gear, Keith Vaughan, Bryan Wynter, Roger Hilton, Ceri Richards, Terry Frost, William Scott, Peter Lanyon, Bernard Cohen, Cecil Stephenson, Henry Cliffe, John

Wells, Ivon Hitchens, Bridget Riley, Patrick Heron, Robyn Denny, John Plumb, Anthony Hill, Pamela Kerr, Sandra Blow, Ian Stephenson, Henry Mundy, and Harold Cohen.

British sculpture had begun to enjoy international repute before 1940, largely through the example of Henry Moore and Barbara Hepworth, who have been mentioned. Contemporary sculptors in England practice an imaginative, expressionist-surrealist or otherwise semiabstract figural art; and there is also a distinctive measure of constructivist-inspired abstraction. The style of Reg Butler's *The Manipulator* (Fig. 120) illustrates a strongly personalized approach to the articulation of both formal and emotional values which impel a generally expressionist manner. Other distinguished contemporaries include F. E. McWilliam, Kenneth Martin, Lynn Chadwick, Kenneth Armitage, Mary Martin, Bernard Meadows, William Turnbull, Robert Adams, John Hoskin, Leslie

Figure 120. Reg Butler. *The Manipulator*, 1954. Bronze, H. 65½". (Courtesy of the Detroit Institute of Arts.)

Figure 121. Marino Marini. *Man on Horseback*, n.d. Bronze, H. 18". (Courtesy of the Detroit Institute of Arts.)

Thornton, Anthony Caro, George Fullard, Hubert Dalwood, Eduardo Paolozzi, Philip King, and Bryan Kneale.

Italian painters and sculptors under the fascist régime of the 1920s and 1930s were not persecuted or given an official program, as were their German contemporaries during the Nazi ascendancy; but they were not encouraged. A school of so-called metaphysical painting and attempts to revitalize futurism resulted in little that was cogent. A few avant-garde strains were kept alive but did not flourish. Since World War II, a refreshing abstract expressionism, in certain hands quite close to the American tradition, has been practiced by Afro Basaldella, Mattia Moreni, Ennio Morlotti, Emilio Vedova, Bruno Cassinari, Renato Birolli, Giuseppi Santomaso, and Alberto Burri. Burri's collages are especially inventive. A more formalized abstraction also abounds.

Recent Italian sculpture has produced both figural and nonfigural trends. Marino Marini (b. 1901) has, since about 1960, developed an increasingly abstract manner; but he is still internationally known for his poignant horsemen (Fig. 121). Marini is Italy's most characteristic modern sculptor.

The figures of Giacomo Manzù, which are very popular, belong to an older tradition. A more vigorous figural expression, some of it approaching abstraction, is that of Marcello Mascherini, Umberto Mastroianni, Emilio Greco, and Mario Negri. Abstraction dominates the works of Mirko Basaldella, Ettore Colla, Alberto Viani, Pietro Consagra, and Berto Lardera.

It is encouraging that in a country with so long and rich a tradition of figural art as Italy, artists can broaden their outlooks beyond a national view and participate with distinction in worldwide trends.

The French corollary of New York action painting, *tachisme,* or art of the spot or touch, appeared in the style of Hans Hartung (b. 1904), a German-born resident of Paris; and it was amplified by another German visitor, Wols (Wolfgang Schultz, 1913–1951). Jean Fautrier, Gerard Schneider, Georges Mathieu, and the Chinese-born Walasse Ting and Zao-Wu-Ki have given *tachisme* individualized interpretation. This style, which was named by the critic Tapié, appears to be closer to American sources, or characteristics, in the art of Camille Bryan, Pierre Soulages, André Lanskoy, Asger Jorn (Danish-born), Tal Coat, and the Canadians Emile Borduas and Jean-Paul Riopelle. Kenzo Okada and Sugai of Japan have made distinctive adaptations of action style and *tachisme.* An abstract art which stands more or less midway between *tachisme* and severer modes is that of Maria Helena Vieira da Silva, who is Portuguese, and Edouard Pignon, Gustave Singier, the late Nicolas de Staël, Richard Mortensen (a Dane), Jean Le Moal, Jean Bazaine, and Roger Bissière. The sharpcut, geometrically based painting of Auguste Herbin and the Italian Alberto Magnelli have sustained the cubist-*De Stijl* tradition in Paris.

French contemporary sculpture is chiefly abstract, or, where figural, conditioned by surrealist, expressionist, and cubist aesthetic. The work of the late distinguished Germaine Richier has been mentioned. Eugène Béothy, Jean Peyrissac, and André Bloc are cubist-constructivist in method. A freer abstraction occurs in the style of François Stahly, Etienne-Martin, Robert Müller, and César. Ossip Zadkine's teaching has been a persistent influence in French sculpture.

Artists in post-World-War-II Germany have had to reconstitute their modern art history. The cultural suppressions of 1933–1945 and the war itself severely deterred the natural growth of a once distinctive tradition. Nevertheless, a number of individual talents have afforded a restored vitality. A mature generation which includes Ernst Wilhelm Nay (b. 1902), Theodore Werner (b. 1886), Conrad Westpfahl (b. 1891), Werner Gilles (b. 1894), Fritz Winter (b. 1906) and the late Willy Baumeister (1889-1955) has produced an imaginative, predominantly abstract, postwar art. The salient influence on most of these men has ultimately proved to be the abstract expressionism of Kandinsky and Klee, not constructivism. Emil Schumacher, Fred Thieler, Winifred Gaul, Karl Götz, Bernhard Schultze, Hann Trier, and Gerhard Hoehme also work in that tradition. A cubist-constructivist influence, not necessarily geometrical, is typical of Rupprecht Geiger, Heinz Trökes, Georg Meistermann, and Rudolf Mauke.

Recent German sculpture has also suffered from the cultural depredations of the 1930s and 1940s. The figural tradition of Barlach, Lehmbruck, Georg Kolbe, and others of combined influences from Rodin or Maillol or expressionism, had continued for some time in the art of Ewald Mataré, Hans Wimmer, Ernesto de Fiori, and Hermann Blumenthal; and imaginative interpretation was still given the figure after the war. Karl Hartung (b. 1908) and Erich Buchholz (b. 1891) have recently worked both representationally and in abstraction. Bernhard Heiliger (b. 1915) has combined abstract expressionist and cubist-constructivist trends in such works as *Change I* (Fig. 122). Hans Uhlmann (b. 1900) is among the clearly constructivist German sculptors. Norbert Kricke (b. 1922) practices an independent, formalized art of sheaflike groupings of steel rods.

An influence which never fully devolved upon German sculpture was that of the strongly original Otto Freundlich (1878–1943), who was working in Paris before the war and died in a concentration camp after sentence by the German occupation authorities in France.

Figure 122. Bernhard Heiliger. *Change I*, 1958. Bronze, H. 28½" with base. (Staempfli Gallery, New York.)

Both Holland and Belgium have vigorously contributed to avantgarde painting and sculpture since about 1950. The Dutch painters, in spite of the international prestige of *De Stijl*, have tended toward an abstract expressionist manner. Karel Appel, Jaap Waagemaker, Lucebert, Gerrit Benner, Bram van Velde, and Ger Lataster belong in most respects to that style. Corneille and Geer van Velde practice a more formalized abstraction. Wessel Couzijn is an outstanding sculptor of the abstract expressionist group.

The Belgian nonfigural painters Henri Michaux, Pierre Alechinsky, Hendrik Werkman, Gaston Bertrand, Louis van Lint, Raoul Ubac, Joseph Lacasse, and Luc Peire are outstanding. An older and independent abtraction has been practiced by Victor Servranckx and Josef Peeters. Raoul d'Haese, Carel Visser, and Reinhoud d'Haese are among the recognized abstract sculptors in Belgium.

Spain long overlooked the contributions of its early modern masters, Picasso, Gris, and Gonzales, but has evolved a significant avantgarde art since the 1940s in the paintings of Juan José Tharrats, Antonio Tapiés, Rafael Conogar, Louis Feíto, and Antonio Saura. Contemporary sculptors include Eduardo Chillada, Angel Ferrant, and José Suirbachs. Recent Spanish painting inclines somewhat more toward abstract expressionism than does the sculpture.

POP; OP

The abstract expressionist movement was still enjoying its great international prestige in the middle 1950s, when newer tendencies appeared in New York. These were not, as is sometimes claimed, reactions against the action style, but were in fact equally avant-garde complements of it. Hard-edge and soft-edge painting; "new image" figures; neo-dada, "combine" art, and assemblages; pop art; and op art have been the principal, more recent developments. Each of them has enjoyed identity as a trend.

It is to be noted that all these styles are closer to abstract expressionism or action art than to earlier modern art, let alone traditional art; and none in effect amounts to a rebuttal of an existing avant-garde manifestation. The hard-edge canvases of Burgoyne Diller, Barnett Newman, Lorser Feitelson, Ellsworth Kelly, Kenneth Noland, and others actually support the integrity of action painting, and, as a new style, action painting aligns itself with the other movements in contradistinction to older forms. The soft-edge paintings of Morris Louis (1912–1962), retaining the bright colors characteristic of hard-edge work but blurring the contours of shapes, are an intriguing conversion of Mark Rothko's action-style rectangles. In Morris' *Number 182* (Fig. 123) the plump, moderately colorful rectangles of Rothko have become attenuated, vertically designed strips of spectrum brilliance. We are confronted, not by opposing concepts, but by remarkably similar ones whose formal components are differently ordered. Similarly, the brutalized, object-like figures of William King and Leonard Baskin are much closer to Willem DeKooning's shattered women than they are to older figural traditions.

Nevertheless, each of the post-abstract-expressionist tendencies is relevant to the history of contemporary art. The arts of assemblage and "combine" styles, which to some extent overlap with one another and with neo-dada and pop, were vigorously and diversely practiced by Richard Stankiewicz, Jason Seley, Robert Watts, Joseph Cornell, Mary Callery, Louise Nevelson, John Chamberlain, Edward Higgins, and others who have sensitively utilized materials ranging from delicately structured, fitted panelings to crushed automotive parts. Lee Bontecou (b. 1931) has contributed to this aesthetic a singularly personal relief or assemblage style, as in her untitled construction in Figure 124.

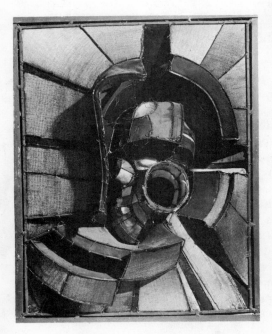

Figure 125. Marisol (Escobar). *Woman and Dog,* 1964. Wood, plastic, liquitex and miscellaneous items, L. 91". (Collection of the Whitney Museum of American Art, New York. Gift of the Friends of the Whitney Museum of American Art.)

Pop art emerged in the mid-1950s out of action and hard-edge painting, neo-dada, assemblage and combine sculpture, and other less distinctive trends. Like dada, which is one of its antecedents, pop has disclosed two broad aspects: one which produces a tangible art of painting, collage, and sculpture or constructions, and a second which involves the arts of human behavior (as in dada public conduct and the creative entertainments of the Cabaret Voltaire group). In its more concrete manifestations, pop has given us a brilliantly ironic *mélange* of painted or drawn representations of commercial packaging and the American comic strip (an art which amused Picasso in early cubist days), stuffed animals on revolving platforms, entire bathroom and bedroom sets, and plaster images modeled directly over clothed persons. Among the outstanding advocates of this art have been Robert Watts, Allan Kaprow, Robert Rauschenberg, Tom Wesselman, Jasper Johns, Roy Lichtenstein, James Rosenquist, Jim Dine, Andy Warhol, Claes Oldenburg, George Segal, and Marisol Escobar. Marisol's *Woman and Dog* (Fig. 125) is an especially characteristic example of the pop cluster of styles. This woman artist, born in Paris of Venezuelan parents, settled in New York in 1950, studying with the abstract expressionist Hans Hofmann.

The behavioral arts of pop are no less remarkable. Creative, but fundamentally disciplined, explosions of antilogical activity are programed by serious artists who studiously avoid identification as theatrical producers or entertainers. These exertions are called "happenings," "events," and "environments." Kaprow, Watts, Dine, and Rauschenberg have developed this field.

Pop art has enjoyed a more or less parallel burgeoning in England, where the form as well as the name may possibly have originated.

Op (optical or retinal art) is a trend of the 1960s which has won acceptance by fashion designers as well as avant-garde practitioners and collectors. It has refined and amplified the principles of geometrical abstraction known to late or flat cubism, *De Stijl*, and constructivism. Angular or curvilinear flat patterns or shallow reliefs are so arranged as to produce interruptions or digressions of the normative optical path, and to result in afterimages of shapes and colors. A distinguished advocate of op is the constructivist-trained, Hungarian-born Victor Vasarely (b. 1908), whose *Eridan II* (Fig. 126) is characteristic. Related

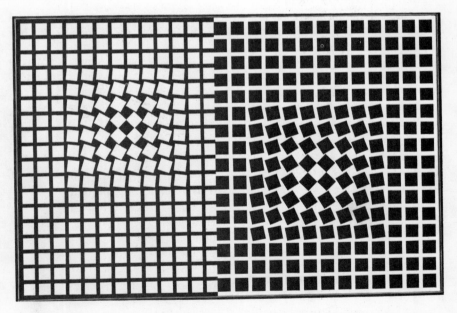

Figure 126. Victor Vasarely. *Eridan II*, 1956. 51 × 76¾". (Courtesy of the Detroit Institute of Arts.)

works were made by the orthodox constructivists at the Bauhaus in
Germany during the 1920s; and Kandinsky, in his own geometrical
style which had developed independently, created very similar ones
in 1927 or earlier. Josef Albers has intensively experimented with
kindred phenomena of design and color, both before and after he
settled in the United States. Some op artists are the Americans Frank
Stella, Tadasky, Gene Davis, Richard Anuskiewicz, Julian Stanczak, and
Jerry Foyster; and Bridget Riley, John Hoyland, and Robyn Denny of
Great Britain.

Some of the modern trends which we have considered will endure,
others will not. This is the inexorable process of art history. But it
is well to remember that skeptics throughout the nineteenth century
and much of the twentieth have mistakenly predicted the early demise
of one valid trend after another; and even briefly significant tendencies in painting and sculpture, past and present, are sometimes relevant
to major developments. Those who have looked upon each new manifestation as a fad forget that cubism and abstract art already enjoy
a longer history as movements than did the predominant style of the
high renaissance in Rome.

Recent modern art has sharpened the perception and enriched
the imagination of man, not because he accepts it or rejects it, but
because it challenges him.

The several kinds of art which painters and sculptors have created
since shortly before 1800 present a remarkable continuum of changing
points of view. These changes have resulted not only from aesthetic
revaluations but also from the response of artists as human beings
to historical developments which have affected or threatened to affect
the society of mankind, of which painters and sculptors, too, are living
components.

It is sometimes said that art is a reflection of the condition of
man. It might well be added that art *is* a condition of man.

bibliography

GENERAL REFERENCES

BARNES, HARRY ELMER, and others, *An Intellectual and Cultural History of the Western World*, 3 vols.; Vol. 3. New York: Dover Publications, Inc., 1965.

BARR, ALFRED H., *Masters of Modern Art*. New York: Museum of Modern Art, 1954.

BELL, CLIVE, *Landmarks in Nineteenth Century Painting*. New York: Harcourt, Brace & Company, 1927.

BERGER, KLAUS, *French Master Drawings of the Nineteenth Century*. New York: Harper & Brothers, 1950.

CHAMBERLIN, MARY, *Guide to Art Reference Books*. New York: American Library Association, 1959.

DIMIER, LOUIS, *Histoire de la peinture au XIXe siècle, 1793-1890*, 2d. ed. Paris: Delgrave, 1926.

ESCHOLIER, RAYMOND, *La peinture française, XIXe siècle*, 2 vols. Paris: Floury, 1941-1943.

GOLDWATER, ROBERT, and MARCO TREVES, *Artists on Art*, 2d. ed. New York: Pantheon, 1947.

GREEN, SAMUEL M., *American Art: A Historical Survey*. New York: The Ronald Press Company, 1966.

HAFTMANN, WERNER, *Painting in the Twentieth Century*. Translated by RALPH MANHEIM, 2 vols. New York: Frederick A. Praeger, Inc., 1961.

HOLT, ELIZABETH, *A Documentary Survey of Art and Architecture in the Nineteenth Century*. Garden City, N.Y.: Doubleday & Company, Inc., 1966.

HUNTER, SAM, *Modern French Painting*. New York: Dell Books, 1956.

LARKIN, OLIVER W., *Art and Life in America*, rev. ed. New York: Holt, Rinehart and Winston, Inc., 1964.

LEYMARIE, JEAN, *French Painting: The Nineteenth Century*. Geneva: Editions d'Art Albert Skira, 1962.

MAILLARD, ROBERT (ed.), *Masterpieces in the History of Painting*. New York: Holt, Rinehart and Winston, Inc., 1961.

MYERS, BERNARD S., *Modern Art in the Making*, 2d. ed. New York: McGraw-Hill Book Company, 1959.

NOVOTNY, FRITZ, *Painting and Sculpture in Europe, 1780-1880*. Baltimore: Penguin Books Inc., 1960.

PELLES, GERALDINE, *Art, Artists, and Society, 1750-1850*. Englewood Cliffs, N.J.: Prentice-Hall, Inc., 1963.

RAYNAL, MAURICE, *History of Modern Painting*, 3 vols. Geneva: Editions d'Art Albert Skira, 1949-1950.

RAVE, PAUL O., *Deutsche Malerei des 19. Jahrhunderts*. Berlin: gebr. Mann, 1949.

RICHARDSON, EDGAR P., *Painting in America*. New York: The Thomas Y. Crowell Co., 1956.

RITCHIE, ANDREW C., *Sculpture of the Twentieth Century*. New York: Museum of Modern Art, 1952.

SELZ, JEAN, *Modern Sculpture: Origins and Evolution*. Translated by ANNETTE MICHELSON. New York: George W. Braziller, Inc., 1963.

SEYMOUR, CHARLES, *Tradition and Experiment in Modern Sculpture*. Washington, D.C.: American University Press, 1949.

SLOANE, JOSEPH C., *French Painting between the Past and the Present*. Princeton, N.J.: Princeton University Press, 1951.

STUBBE, WOLF, *Graphic Arts in the Twentieth Century*. New York: Frederick A. Praeger, Inc., 1963.

SWEENEY, JAMES J., *Plastic Redirections in Twentieth Century Painting*. Chicago: Unversity of Chicago Press, 1934.

TRIER, EDUARD, *Moderne Plastik von Auguste Rodin bis Marino Marini*. Frankfurt-am-Main: Büchergilde Gütenberg, 1955.

WILENSKI, REGINALD H., *Modern French Painters*. New York: Harcourt, Brace & Company, 1949 (and 2 vols., New York: Vintage Books, Inc., 1960).

CHAPTER 1

Arts Yearbook, II (1958) (number devoted to romantic art).

BAUDELAIRE, CHARLES, *The Mirror of Art*. Translated by JONATHAN MAYNE. Garden City, N.Y.: Doubleday & Co., Inc., 1956.

BAZIN, GERMAIN, *Corot*. Paris: Tisné, 1951.

BERGER, KLAUS, *Géricault and His Work*. Lawrence: University of Kansas Press, 1955.

BLANC, CHARLES, *Histoire des peintres de toutes les écoles*, 14 vols. Paris: Renouard, 1861-1870.

BOAS, GEORGE (ed.), *Courbet and the Naturalistic Movement*. Baltimore: The Johns Hopkins University Press, 1938.

BOASE, T. S. R., *English Art, 1800-1870*. London: Oxford University Press, 1959.

BRION, MARCEL, *Art of the Romantic Era*. New York: Frederick A. Praeger, Inc., 1966.

COURTHION, PIERRE, *David, Ingres, Gros, et Géricault*. Geneva: Editions d'Art Albert Skira, 1946.

DELACROIX, EUGÈNE, *The Journal of Eugène Delacroix*. Translated and edited by WALTER PACH. New York: Crown Publishers, 1948.

DOWD, DAVID L., *Pageant-Master of the Republic: Jacques-Louis David and the French Revolution*. Lincoln: University of Nebraska Press, 1948.

FERRARI, ENRIQUE L., *Goya: His Complete Etchings, Aquatints and Lithographs*. New York: Harry N. Abrams, Inc., 1962.

FINBERG, ALEXANDER J., *The Life of J. M. W. Turner, R. A.*, revised ed. Oxford: Clarendon Press, 1961.

FOÇILLON, HENRI, *La peinture au XIXe siècle: Le retour à l'antique; Le romantisme*. Paris: Laurens, 1927.

FRIEDLAENDER, WALTER, *David to Delacroix*. Translated by ROBERT GOLD-WATER. Cambridge: Harvard University Press, 1952.

GAUTIER, THÉOPHILE, *Histoire du romantisme*, 3rd ed. Paris: Charpentier, 1877.

HERBERT, ROBERT L., *Barbizon Revisited*. New York: Clarke and Way, 1963.

HUYGHE, RENÉ, *Delacroix*. Translated by JONATHAN GRIFFIN. New York: Harry N. Abrams, Inc., 1963.

KEY, SYDNEY J., *John Constable, His Life and Work*. London: Phoenix House, Ltd., 1948.

LASSAIGNE, JACQUES, *Eugène Delacroix*. New York: Harper & Brothers, 1950.

LÉGER, CHARLES, *Courbet*. Paris: Crés, 1929.

LOPEZ-REY, JOSÉ, *Francisco Goya*. New York: Harper & Brothers, 1950.

MACK, GERSTLE, *Gustave Courbet*. New York: Alfred A. Knopf, Inc., 1935.

MILLER, MARGARET, "Géricault's Paintings of the Insane," *Journal of the Warburg and Courtauld Institutes*, IV: 151-163, 1940-1941.

PACH, WALTER, "The Heritage of J.-L. David," *Gazette des Beaux-Arts*, XLV: 103-112, 1955.

———, *Ingres*. New York: Harper & Brothers, 1939.

RAYNAL, MAURICE, *The Nineteenth Century: From Goya to Gauguin*. Translated by JAMES EMMONS. Geneva: Editions d'Art Albert Skira, 1951.

RITCHIE, ANDREW C., "The Evolution of Ingres' Portrait of the Comtesse d'Haussonville." *Art Bulletin*, XXII: 119-126, 1940.

SCHAPIRO, MEYER, "Courbet and Popular Imagery, an Essay on Realism and Naiveté." *Journal of the Warburg and Courtauld Institutes*, IV: 164-191, 1940-1941.

SCHLENOFF, NORMAN, *Ingres: Ses sources littéraires*. Paris: Presses Universitaires de France, 1956.

SENSIER, ALFRED, *Jean François Millet, Peasant and Painter*. Translated by HELENA DE KAY. Boston: Osgood, 1881.

WILDENSTEIN, GEORGES, *Ingres*. London: Phaidon Press Ltd., Publishers, 1954.

CHAPTER 2

ADHÉMAR, JEAN, *Honoré Daumier*. Paris: Tisné, 1954.

DURET, THÉODORE, *Manet and the French Impressionists*. Translated by J. E. C. FLITCH. Philadelphia: J. B. Lippincott Company, 1910.

FRANCASTEL, PIERRE, "La Fin de l'impressionisme: Esthétique et causalité," in *Studies in Western Art: Problems of the Nineteenth and Twentieth Centuries*, ed. MILLARD MEISS. Princeton, N.J.: Princeton University Press, 1963, pp. 122-133.

HAMILTON, GEORGE H., *Manet and His Critics*. New Haven, Conn.: Yale University Press, 1954.

LASSAIGNE, JACQUES, *Daumier*. Translated by EVELINE B. SHAW. London: Wm. Heinemann, 1938.

LEYMARIE, JEAN, *Impressionism*. Translated by JAMES EMMONS, 2 vols. New York: Skira, Inc., Publishers, and Geneva: Editions d'Art Albert Skira, 1955.

RAYNAL, MAURICE, *History of Modern Painting: From Baudelaire to Bonnard*. Geneva: Editions d'Art Albert Skira, 1949.

REWALD, JOHN, *History of Impressionism*, revised ed. New York: Museum of Modern Art, 1961.

RICH, DANIEL C., *Degas*. New York: Harry N. Abrams, Inc., 1951.

SEITZ, WILLIAM, *Claude Monet*. New York: Harry N. Abrams, Inc., 1960.

VENTURI, LIONELLO, *Les Archives de l'impressionisme*, 2 vols. Paris and New York: Durand-Ruel, 1939.

WECHSLER, HERMAN J., *French Impressionists and Their Circle*. New York: Harry N. Abrams, Inc., 1955.

CHAPTER 3

BAUR, JOHN I. H., *American Painting in the Nineteenth Century: Main Trends and Movements*. New York: Frederick A. Praeger, Inc., 1953.

BENESCH, OTTO, *Edvard Munch*. London: Phaidon Press, Ltd., Publishers, 1960.

CÉZANNE, PAUL, *Letters*, ed., JOHN REWALD. London: Bruno Cassirer, Publishers, Ltd., 1941.

DENIS, MAURICE, *Théories, 1890-1910*, 4th ed. Paris: Rouart et Watelin, 1920.

DEKNATEL, FREDERICK B., *Edvard Munch*. Boston: Institute of Contemporary Art, 1950.

FRY, ROGER, *Cézanne: A Study of His Development*. London: L. & V. Woolf, 1927.

GAUGUIN, PAUL, *Intimate Journals*. Translated by VAN WYCK BROOKS. New York: Crown Publishers, 1936.

GOLDSCHEIDER, LUDWIG, *Vincent Van Gogh*. London: Phaidon Press, Ltd., Publishers, 1947.

GOLDWATER, ROBERT, *Gauguin*. New York: Harry N. Abrams, Inc., 1956.

HOMER, WILLIAM I., *Seurat and the Science of Painting*. Cambridge: Massachusetts Institute of Technology Press, 1964.

LANCASTER, CLAY, "Oriental Contributions to Art Nouveau," *Art Bulletin* XXXIV: 300-301, 1952.

LENNING, HENRY F., *The Art Nouveau*. The Hague: Nijhoff, 1951.

MADSEN, STEPHEN T., *Sources of Art Nouveau*. New York: George Wittenborn, Inc., 1956.

MEIER-GRAEFE, JULIUS, *Vincent Van Gogh: A Biographical Study*. Translated by JOHN H. REECE. New York: Harcourt, Brace & Company, 1933.

MEISS, MILLARD (ed.), *Studies in Western Art*, 4 vols.; Vol. 4 *Problems of the Nineteenth and Twentieth Centuries*. Princeton, N.J.: Princeton University Press, 1963.

NOVOTNY, FRITZ, *Cézanne*. London: Phaidon Press, Ltd., Publishers, 1948.

———, "The Reaction Against Impressionism from the Artistic Point of View," in *Problems of the Nineteenth and Twentieth Centuries*, ed. MILLARD MEISS. Princeton, N.J.: Princeton University Press, 1963, pp. 93-103.

REWALD, JOHN, *Post-Impressionism: From Van Gogh to Gauguin*. New York: Museum of Modern Art, 1956.

SCHAPIRO, MEYER, *Van Gogh*. New York: Harry N. Abrams, Inc., 1950.

——, *Paul Cézanne*. New York: Harry N. Abrams, Inc., 1952.

——, "New Light on Seurat." *Art News* LVII: 22-24, April, 1958.

SCHMUTZLER, ROBERT, *Art Nouveau*. Translated by EDOUARD RODITI. New York: Harry N. Abrams, Inc., 1962.

SELZ, PETER, *Art Nouveau*. New York: Doubleday & Co., Inc., 1959.

SIGNAC, PAUL, *D'Eugène Delacroix au néoimpressionisme*, 4th ed. Paris: Floury, 1939 (first published 1899).

SWEET, FREDERICK A., *Sargent, Whistler, and Mary Cassatt*. Chicago: Art Institute of Chicago, 1954.

CHAPTER 4

ARSÈNE, ALEXANDRE, *Antoine Louis Barye*. Paris: Librairie de l'Art, 1889.

BARR, MARGUERITE, S., *Medardo Rosso*. New York: Museum of Modern Art, 1964.

CLEMENT-CARPEAUX, LOUISE, *La vérité sur l'oeuvre et la vie de J.-B. Carpeaux*, 2 vols. Paris: Dousset et Bigerelle, 1935.

CLARIS, EDMOND, *De l'impressionisme en sculpture*. Paris: Editions de la Nouvelle Revue, 1902.

ELSEN, ALBERT E., *Rodin*. New York: Museum of Modern Art, 1963.

HILDEBRAND, ADOLF VON, *The Problem of Form*. Translated by MAX MEYER and R. M. OGDEN. New York: J. E. Stechert & Company, 1907 (first published as *Problem der Form in der bildenden Kunst*, Strassbourg, 1893).

JEAN-BAPTISTE CARPEAUX (exhibition catalog). Paris: Musée du Petit Palais, 1955.

LAMI, STANISLAS, *Dictionnaire des sculpteurs de l'école française au XIXe siècle*, 4 vols. Paris: Champion, 1914-1921.

REWALD, JOHN, *Complete Degas Sculpture*. New York: Harry N. Abrams, Inc., 1957.

STORY, SOMMERVILLE, *Auguste Rodin*. New York: Phaidon Press Ltd., Publishers, 1951.

SUTTON, DENYS, *Rodin*. London: Penguin Books, Ltd., 1963.

TAFT, LORADO, *History of American Sculpture*, revised ed. New York: The Macmillan Company, 1930.

VALENTINER, WILHELM R., *Origins of Modern Sculpture*. New York: George Wittenborn, Inc., 1932.

CHAPTER 5

AMERICAN ABSTRACT ARTISTS, *World of Abstract Art*. New York: George Wittenborn, Inc., 1957.

APOLLINAIRE, GUILLAUME, *The Cubist Painters*, 2nd ed. Translated by LIONEL ABEL. New York: George Wittenborn, Inc., 1949.

ARNHEIM, RUDOLPH, *Picasso's Guernica: The Genesis of a Painting*. Berkeley: University of California Press, 1962.

BALLO, GUIDO, *Modern Italian Painting*. New York: Frederick A. Praeger, Inc., 1958.

BARR, ALFRED H., *Picasso: Fifty Years of His Art*. New York: Museum of Modern Art, 1946.

——, *Fantastic Art, Dada, Surrealism*. New York: Museum of Modern Art, 1947.

——, *Matisse, His Art and His Public*. New York: Museum of Modern Art, 1951.

BAUR, JOHN I. H., *Revolution and Tradition in Modern American Art*. Cambridge, Mass.: Harvard University, 1951.

BERCKELAERS, FERDINAND (see SEUPHOR, MICHEL).

BOWNESS, ALAN, *Modern Sculpture*. New York: Dutton, 1965.

BROWN, MILTON, *American Painting from the Armory Show to the Depression*. Princeton, N.J.: Princeton University Press, 1955.

BUCHHEIM, LOTHAR GÜNTHER, *The Graphic Art of German Expressionism*. New York: Universe Books, Inc., 1960.

CLOUGH, ROSA T., *Futurism: The Story of a Modern Art Movement*. New York: Wisdom Library, 1961.

CRESPELLE, JEAN P., *The Fauves*. Translated by ANITA BROOKNER. Greenwich, Conn.: New York Graphic Society, 1962.

ELGAR, FRANK, and MAILLARD, ROBERT, *Picasso*. New York: Frederick A. Praeger, Inc., 1956.

GALLOWAY, JOHN, *Origins of Modern Art, 1905-1914*. New York: McGraw-Hill Book Company, 1965.

GAMBILLO, MARIA DRUDI, and FIORI, TERESA, *Archivi del Futurismo*. Rome: De Luca Editore, 1958.

GASCOYGNE, DAVID, *A Short Survey of Surrealism*. London: R. Cobden-Sanderson, Ltd., 1935.

GIEDION, SIEGFRIED, *Walter Gropius: Work and Teamwork*. New York: Reinhold Publishing Corporation, 1954.

GIEDION-WELCKER, CAROLA, *Contemporary Sculpture*, revised ed. New York: George Wittenborn, 1961.

GOLDING, JOHN, *Cubism: A History and An Analysis, 1907-1959*. New York: George Wittenborn, Inc., 1959.

GOLDWATER, ROBERT, *Primitivism in Modern Painting*. New York: Harper & Brothers, 1938.

GOODRICH, LLOYD, and BAUR, JOHN I. H., *American Art of Our Century*, New York: Frederick A. Praeger, Inc., 1961.

GRAY, CAMILLA, *The Great Experiment in Russian Art, 1863-1922*. New York: Harry N. Abrams, Inc., 1962.

GROHMANN, WILL, *Wassily Kandinsky*. New York: Harry N. Abrams, Inc., 1958.

HAFTMANN, WERNER, *Painting in the Twentieth Century*, 2 vols. Translated by RALPH MANHEIM. New York: Frederick A. Praeger, Inc., 1961.

HAFTMANN, WERNER; HENTZEN, ALFRED; and LIBERMAN, WILLIAM S. *German Art of the Twentieth Century*. New York: Museum of Modern Art, 1957.

HOFFMANN, EDITH, *Kokoschka, His Life and Work*. London: Faber & Faber, Ltd., 1947.

HOFMANN, WERNER, *Lehmbruck*. New York: Universe Books, Inc., 1959.

HOPE, HENRY, *Georges Braque*. New York: Museum of Modern Art, 1949.

HUNTER, SAM, *Modern American Painting and Sculpture*. New York: Dell Books, 1959.

JANIS, SIDNEY, *Abstract and Surrealist Art in America*. New York: Reynal & Hitchcock, 1944.

JEAN, MARCEL, *The History of Surrealist Painting*. Translated by S. W. TAYLOR. New York: Grove Press, Inc., 1960.

KAHNWEILER, DANIEL H., *The Rise of Cubism*. Translated by HENRY ARONSON. New York: George Wittenborn, Inc., 1949.

KANDINSKY, WASSILY, *Concerning the Spiritual in Art*. Translated by MICHAEL SADLEIR and others. New York: George Wittenborn, Inc., 1947.

KLEE, PAUL, *Pedagogical Sketchbook*. Translated by SIBYL MOHOLY-NAGY. New York: Frederick A. Praeger, 1953

KUH, KATHERINE, *Léger*. Chicago: Art Institute of Chicago, 1953.

LANGUI, EMILE, *Fifty Years of Modern Art*. New York: Frederick A. Praeger, Inc., 1959.

LARREA, JUAN, *Guernica*. New York: Curt Valentin, 1947.

MAILLARD, ROBERT (ed.), *Dictionary of Modern Sculpture*. Translated by BETTINA WADIA. New York: Tudor Publishing Company, 1960.

MALEVICH, KASIMIR, *The Non-Objective World*. Translated by HOWARD DEARSTYNE. Chicago: Theobald & Co., Publishers, 1959.

MONDRIAN, PIET, *Plastic Art and Pure Plastic Art*. New York: George Wittenborn, Inc., 1945.

MOTHERWELL, ROBERT, *The Dada Painters and Poets*. New York: George Wittenborn, Inc., 1951.

MYERS, BERNARD S., *The German Expressionists: A Generation in Revolt*. New York: Frederick A. Praeger, Inc., 1957.

NACENTA, RAYMOND, *School of Paris: The Artistic Climate of Paris Since 1910*. Greenwich, Conn.: New York Graphic Society, 1960.

PENROSE, ROLAND, *Picasso: His Life and Work*. London: Harper & Brothers, 1959 (also, New York: Schocken Books, Inc., 1962).

READ, HERBERT, *A Concise History of Modern Sculpture*. London: Thames and Hudson, Ltd., 1964.

——, SYLVESTER, DAVID, and BOWNESS, ALAN, *Henry Moore: Sculpture and Drawings*, 3 vols. London: Percy Lund, Humphries & Co., Ltd., 1965.

RITCHIE, ANDREW C., *Aristide Maillol*. Buffalo: Albright Art Gallery, 1945.

——, *Abstract Painting and Sculpture in America*. New York: Museum of Modern Art, 1951.

——, *The New Decade*. New York: Museum of Modern Art, 1955.

ROSENBLUM, ROBERT, *Cubism and Twentieth Century Art*. New York: Harry N. Abrams, Inc., 1961.

SCHAEFER-SIMMERN, HENRY, *Sculpture in Europe Today*. Berkeley: University of California Press, 1955.

SELZ, PETER, *German Expressionist Painting*. Berkeley: University of California Press, 1957.

SEUPHOR, MICHEL, *Piet Mondrian: Life and Work*. New York: Harry N. Abrams, Inc., 1956.

——, *The Sculpture of This Century.* Translated by HAAKON CHEVALIER. New York: George W. Braziller, Inc., 1961.
SOBY, JAMES T., *Modigliani; Paintings, Drawings, Sculpture.* New York: Museum of Modern Art, 1951.
——, *Giorgio de Chirico.* New York: Museum of Modern Art, 1955.
——, and BARR, ALFRED H., *Twentieth Century Italian Art.* New York: Museum of Modern Art, 1949.
TAYLOR, JOSHUA C., *Futurism.* New York: Museum of Modern Art, 1961.
VERKAUF, WILLY (ed.), *Dada: Monograph of a Movement.* New York: George Wittenborn, Inc., 1957.
WINGLER, HANS M., *Der blaue Reiter.* Feldafing: Buchheim, 1954.
ZERVOS, CHRISTIAN, *Picasso.* Paris: Editions *Cahiers d'Art*, vols. I-XII, 1932-1961.

CHAPTER 6

ALLOWAY, LAWRENCE, "Notes on Op Art," in GREGORY BATTCOCK (ed.), *The New Art.* New York: E. P. Dutton & Co., Inc., 1966, pp. 83-91.
Art Since 1945. New York: Harry N. Abrams, Inc., 1958.
BARR, ALFRED H., "Gorky, DeKooning, Pollock," *Art News* XLIX: 22-23, 1950.
BATTCOCK, GREGORY (ed.), *The New Art.* New York: E. P. Dutton & Co., Inc., 1966.
GREENBERG, CLEMENT, "The Present Prospects of American Painting and Sculpture," *Horizon,* Nos. 93-94, 1947.
HAMMACHER, A. M., *The Dutch Contribution to the International Development of Arts Since 1945.* Amsterdam: Stedelijk Museum, 1962.
HESS, THOMAS B., *Abstract Painting, Background and American Phase.* New York: The Viking Press, Inc., 1951.
——, *Willem DeKooning.* New York: George W. Braziller, Inc., 1959.
HUNTER, SAM, "Jackson Pollock," *Museum of Modern Art Bulletin,* XXIV: 4-36, 1956-1957.
KAPROW, ALLAN, *Assemblage, Environments, and Happenings.* New York: Harry N. Abrams, Inc., 1966.
MILLER, DOROTHY C., *Twelve Americans.* New York: Museum of Modern Art, 1956.
O'HARA, FRANK, *Jackson Pollock.* New York: George W. Braziller, Inc., 1959.
PONENTE, NELLO, *Modern Painting: Contemporary Trends.* Translated by JAMES EMMONS. Geneva: Editions d'Art Albert Skira, 1960.
POUSETTE-DART, NATHANIEL, *Amercian Painting Today.* New York: Hastings House, 1956.
ROSENBERG, HAROLD, *The Tradition of the New.* New York: Horizon Books, 1959.
ROBLOWSKY, JOHN, and HEYMAN, K., *Pop Art.* New York: Basic Books, 1965.
SCHAPIRO, MEYER, "The Younger American Painters of Today," *The Listener,* No. 1404, January, 1956, pp. 146-147.
——, "On the Humanity of Abstract Painting," in *Proceedings of the American Academy of Arts and Letters,* 2d. Series, No. 10, 1960.
SCHWABACHER, ETHEL K., *Arshile Gorky.* New York: The Macmillan Company, 1957.

SEITZ, WILLIAM, *The Responsive Eye*. New York: Museum of Modern
    Art, 1965.
STEINBERG, LEO, "Contemporary Art and the Plight of its Public," in GREGORY
    BATTCOCK (ed.), *The New Art*. New York: E. P. Dutton & Co., Inc.,
    1966, pp. 27-57.
TILLIM, SIDNEY, "Optical Art: Pending or Ending?" *Arts* XXXIX, 1965.

index

Modern Art

JOHN GALLOWAY. John Galloway is a professor of art history and chairman of the department of art at Oakland University. He received his B.A. and M.A. degrees at American University and Ph.D. from Columbia University. He has studied painting in Washington, D. C., and was a senior research scholar under the Fulbright Act during which time he studied modern and primitive art in several European countries.

Previous teaching positions include The American University, University of Alabama, Indiana University, and Southern Illinois University.

Photo by Spence Galloway

The Brown
studies in art series

- **CLASSICAL ART**   R. L. Bohr, Sacramento State
- **THE ART OF THE ITALIAN RENAISSANCE**   Edmund Eglinski, University of Kansas
- **MODERN ART: THE NINETEENTH AND TWENTIETH CENTURIES**   John C. Galloway, Oakland University, Rochester, Michigan
- **FORMS OF ART**   Peter Gilleran, Wayne State University, Detroit
- **AMERICAN ART**   David Gebhard, University of California, Santa Barbara
- **VISUAL ART IN GLASS**   Dominick Labino
- **POTTERY**   Charles Lakofsky, Bowling Green University
- **ASIAN ART**   John D. La Plante, Stanford University
- **THE ART OF THE PRINT**   Earl G. Mueller, Duke University
- **ART IN COMMERCE AND INDUSTRY**   Robert C. Niece, Art Center College of Design, Los Angeles, California
- **ANCIENT NEAR EAST ART**   Robert H. Rough, Michigan State University
- **MEDIEVAL ART**   Norris K. Smith, Washington University
- **SEVENTEENTH- AND EIGHTEENTH-CENTURY ART**   Robert Stinson, Bowling Green University
- **RENAISSANCE ART OUTSIDE ITALY**   Marilyn Stokstad, University of Kansas
- **PREHISTORIC ART**   Frederick O. Waage, Cornell University
- **CRAFTS AND CRAFTSMEN**   Irwin Whitaker, Michigan State University
- **PHOTOGRAPHY**

WM. C. BROWN COMPANY PUBLISHERS

Dubuque, Iowa